Birds & Mammals
of the Antarctic, Subantarctic & Falkland Islands

Frank S. Todd

San Diego
Natural History Museum

Ibis Publishing Company

Birds & Mammals of the Antarctic,
Subantarctic & Falkland Islands

©2004 Frank S. Todd

Ibis Publishing Company
44970 Via Renaissance
Temecula, California 92590
E-mail: ibispub@msn.com

Library of Congress Catalog Number pending

ISBN Number 0-934797-22-6

Design and layout by John and Lisa Bass

Printed in Korea

I

TABLE OF CONTENTS

PREFACE AND ACKNOWLEDGEMENTS IV
MAP 2

BIRDS

PENGUINS 4
GREATER ALBATROSSES 16
MOLLYMAWK ALBATROSSES 21
SOOTY ALBATROSSES 27
GIANT-PETRELS 29
PETRELS 30
SHEARWATERS 37
PRIONS 39
STORM-PETRELS 42
DIVING-PETRELS 45
CORMORANTS (SHAGS) 46
WATERFOWL (DUCKS, GEESE AND SWANS) 49
BIRDS OF PREY 52
RAILS 52
SHEATHBILLS 53
SHOREBIRDS (WADERS) 54
GULLS, TERNS AND SKUAS 55
PARAKEETS 60
PASSERINES 61
INTRODUCED NEW ZEALAND EXOTICS 64
WINTERING BIRDS AND VAGRANTS (ILLUSTRATED) 66
WINTERING BIRDS AND VAGRANTS (NON-ILLUSTRATED) 74

MAMMALS

FUR SEALS, SEA LIONS AND SEALS 76
DOLPHINS AND PORPOISES 83
TOOTHED WHALES 86
BALEEN WHALES 91
INTRODUCED MAMMALS 97

FALKLAND ISLANDS BIRDS

BREEDING BIRDS 100
WINTERING BIRDS AND VAGRANTS (ILLUSTRATED) 120
WINTERING BIRDS AND VAGRANTS (NON-ILLUSTRATED) 131

APPENDIX 132
INDEX 135

To Suzy & Chris

Far better it is to dare mighty things, to win glorious triumphs
even though checkered by failure, than to take rank with those
poor spirits who neither enjoy much nor suffer much because
they live in the gray twilight that knows not victory nor defeat

Theodore Roosevelt
26th U.S. President
Rough Rider
Sportsman
Conservationist

PREFACE

This handbook is primarily for the novice bird and marine mammal watcher, though serious birders will hopefully benefit as well. All birds and mammals likely to be encountered on a southern sea voyage are illustrated, though not necessarily to scale. Brief written descriptions accompany most seabird and all marine mammal images, but this was deemed unnecessary for island endemics where there is no possibility of confusion with other species.

Penguins are symbolic of the far south, with 14 of the 17 species frequenting the region, though only two (Emperor and Adélie) are essentially restricted to the frozen southern continent. Little and Fiordland Crested Penguins just reach the Snares or Auckland Islands as vagrants. While not inhabitants of the Antarctic or Subantarctic, the three northern penguins (Galapagos, Humboldt and African) have been included because their existence depends entirely on cold-water currents spawned in Antarctica.

Seabird identification has been greatly complicated in recent years due to the tendency to elevate subspecific forms to full species level, based primarily on DNA analysis and nesting zoogeography. Lance Tickell perhaps sums it up best in his monograph on albatrosses when he sagely notes "As the science of systematics advances, ornithologists and birders encounter difficulties when their measurements, or the plumage and behavior they observe, cease to be the characters used by taxonomists to determine species. Not long ago, most biologists could take part in taxonomic debate with some confidence. Now, short of retraining in biochemistry and cladistics, many are obliged to adopt an act of faith in the latest technology." The minor differences in some of these new 'species' can be so subtle that it is highly unlikely that any but the most experienced seabird specialist could accurately separate them at sea, and even the experts admittedly experience difficulty. To be absolutely positive of the identity of some species, the bird in question must either be observed on the nest or subjected to a DNA sample. Obviously the latter is well beyond the capability of most people, thus I have been rather reluctant to fully embrace the new trend, generally adhering to the more traditional taxonomic scheme in which most forms are retained at subspecific level.

For most people balancing precariously on a wildly bouncing deck in stormy seas amid spray-filled air, merely being able to identify a small bird erratically darting about as a prion is challenge enough— never mind the specific species. The six, or even seven, species of prions, as well as the two southern diving-petrels, generally must be examined in the hand to accurately ascertain the species, and even then confusion often prevails. Fortunately the six very similar shags in the 'blue-eyed' shag complex are essentially restricted to specific islands, thus a shag observed on Heard Island is most likely a Heard Shag. However, in the final analysis, merely being able to separate a Wandering Albatross from a very similar Royal Albatross is probably sufficient for most of us.

Since 1994, between 50,000 and 100,000 albatrosses and large petrels have perished annually by longliners when feeding birds pounce upon baited hooks and are dragged down to the depths and drown. Most albatrosses are killed by Patagonian Toothfish longliners operating in southern waters, but female Wandering Albatrosses tend to forage farther north where they are vulnerable to the Bluefin Tuna longline fishery. For every breeding bird killed, an egg or chick also perishes because eggs or chicks cannot be cared for by a single parent. Due to such scandalous mortality, many albatross populations have declined substantially over the past 30 years, with some presently very much at risk. Greater albatrosses (Wandering, Royal and Amsterdam) in particular have exceedingly slow reproductive rates, with most not successfully breeding until 10 or more years of age, and at best fledge but a single chick every other year. Such low productivity is normally offset by great longevity; indeed, the greatest documented age for any wild bird is a female Northern Royal Albatross that survived at least 60 years. While most legal longliners are committed to reducing seabird mortality, there may be as many as ten times the number of pirate vessels fishing illegally in southern waters than legal boats. Even if longlining mortality terminated today, it would take decades for some populations to recover. The *Save the Albatross Foundation* has been leading the fight to curtail this senseless slaughter and should be supported by all who appreciate seabirds.

ACKNOWLEDGEMENTS

Much of the credit for this book goes to Naidine Adams Larsen, who almost single-handedly kept the project viable when the path was poorly illuminated. Charlie Rumford (Mary H. Rumsey Foundation), Lars and Erica Wikander (Quark Expeditions), Jorge Jordan, Harry G. & Pauline M. Austin Foundation, International Wild Waterfowl Association, Pony Duke and Irwin Bell all awarded grants.

Countless shipmates and valued colleagues contributed enormously in numerous ways over the years. A mere handful of these include Susan Adie and Brad Stal, Thomas Bachman, Pete and Jennifer Clement, John Croxall (BAS), Tui De Roy and Mark Jones, Conrad and Carmen Field, Art Ford, Bob Headland, Brent Houston (Lindblad Expeditions), Jerry Kooyman, Denise Landau and Dick Filby, Peter Harrison and Shirley Metz, Rod Ledingham, Colin Monteath, Mike McDowell, Barrie McKelvey, Mike Messick, Ron Naveen, Bob Pitman and Lisa Ballance, Julio Preller, Randall Reeves, Paula Olson, Tony and Tim Soper, John Splettstoesser, Werner Stambach, Brent Stewart and Pam Yochem, Charles Swithinbank, Victoria (Underwood) and Charlie Wheatley, Don Walsh, Lars and Erica Wikander, and Jane Wilson. Fabrice Genevois was especially helpful, including proofing and even having the bird and mammal names translated into French, German and Spanish, with much assistance from Betsy Pincheira and Sylvia Stevens.

The tireless efforts of Joe and Sally DeSarro cannot be overstated. Michael and Judy Steinhardt, John Chandler, Fred, Sue, Lars and Carol Morris, Flip Nicklin, Larry

Minden (Mindon Pictures), Mike and Ali Lubbock, and Scott and Cory Drieschman all were extremely supportive. The captains, crew and staff of the many ships I have sailed on made it possible to often accomplish the seemingly impossible. For the past 15 years, I have mainly been aboard Russian vessels, under the command of Captains Petr Golikov, Victor Vasil'yev and Andrey Gostnikov.

The New Zealand Department of Conservation (DOC/*Te Papa Atawhai*) was of incalculable aid and the project would have been far more difficult without the considerable efforts of Rob McCallum, Belinda Sawyer and Ferne McKenzie in particular, as well as Bob Dixon, Pete McCelland, Lou Sanson, Tom Hopkins, Paul van Klink and Glen Newton. In the Falkland Islands, my dear friends Tony and Kim Chater provided immeasurable help, with Rob and Lorraine McGill, Lewis Clifton, Rod and Lily Napier and Robin Woods also assisting in many ways. In Africa, Jan Kennedy, Johan Visagie (Dassen Island/Western Cape Nature Conservation Board), Peter Ryan, Bruce Dyer, John Cooper and Anton Wolfaardt all contributed greatly. Jorge Jordan, Betsy Pincheira, Michel Durant and Braulio Araya made my life considerably easier in South America. The creative and highly skilled John and Lisa Bass worked tirelessly on the book design and stunning layouts. Jim and Karen Clements of Ibis Publishing Company and the San Diego Natural History Museum were of great help. My daughter and son-in-law, Suzy and Chris Johnson, made it possible for me to spend extended periods of time in the field.

While most images are my own, many naturalists and photographers gave freely of their time and expertise. Pictures by other photographers are designated by their initials next to their image: Alain Bidart(AB), Charles André Bost(CAB), Dennis Buurman(DB), Tony Chater(TC), David Cothram/Lindblad Expeditions(DC), Paul Ensor(PE), Fabrice Genevois(FG), Martin Hale(MH), Peter Harrison(PH), Derek Hatch(DH), Brent Houston(BH), Joe Jehl(JJ), Frédéric Jiguet(FJ), Jerry Kooyman(JK), Benoît Lequette(BL), Teus Luijendijk(TL), Flip Nicklin(FN)*, Paula Olson (PO), Tony Palliser(TP), Robert Pitman(RP), Peter Ryan(PR), Arnold Small(AS), Edgar Spanhauer(ES), Brent Stewart(BS), Sea World(SW), Barbara Todd(BT) Ingrid Visser(IV) and Barbara Weinecke(BW).

New Zealand Department of Conservation (DOC): R. Anderson(RA), Andrea Booth(AB/DOC), Jeremy Carroll(JC), Wynston Cooper(WC), Andy Cox(AC), Dave Crouchley(DC/DOC), D. Garrick(DG), Terry C. Greene(TG), J. L. Kendrick(JLK), Chris Smuts-Kennedy(CSK), Pete McClelland(PM), Peter J. Moore(PJM), Rod Morris(RM), Don Merton(DM), Peter Morrison(PM/DOC), Andrew Penniket(AP), Peter Reese(PR/DOC), C. J. R. Robinson(CR), T. Smith(TS), M. F. Soper(MFS). Graeme A. Taylor(GT), Glen Tomlinson(GT/DOC), Dick Veitch(DV), M. J. Williams(MW) and A. Wright(AW).

Peter Harrison(PH) graciously painted several of the more elusive petrel species and Kim Chater(KC) painted the Sei Whale.
*Obtained under NMFS permit

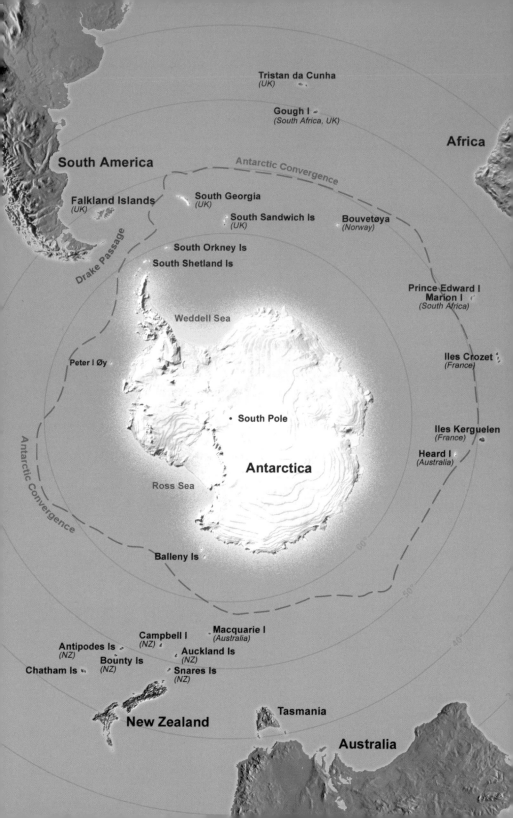

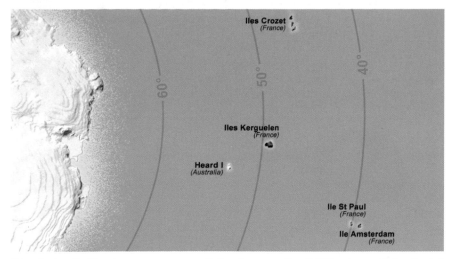

The Antarctic Treaty encompasses all territory south of 60°, where all territorial claims are frozen, thus making Antarctica the only international continent. While the political boundary lies at 60° S, the Antarctic Convergence or Antarctic Polar Front represents the biological or oceanographic boundary. Normally located between 55° and 60° S, the variable latitudinal position of the convergence shifts seasonally, vacillating nearly 100 miles (160km) north and south. Within the convergence zone, warmer, more saline subtropical currents flowing south collide with northward-moving, colder, denser and less salty polar water. The broad invisible boundary of this well-defined oceanic frontal system is characterized by an up-welling due to the colliding masses of warm and cold water that churn nutrients and food to the surface. This nutrient-enriched up-welling is an especially rich feeding ground for a profusion of foraging seabirds and cetaceans. Most Subantarctic islands lie just north or south of the convergence, but a few, such as Gough, Tristan da Cunha, Amsterdam and St Paul Islands, are well to the north, though much of the avifauna nesting on these islands is clearly Subantarctic.

Breeding ranges are listed for most nesting birds, but seabirds wander extensively and often occur well away from breeding islands. Many seabirds, especially albatrosses, are particularly numerous between 40° and 65° S, where uninterrupted winds circulate vigorously around the globe. These latitudes of the notorious roaring forties, furious fifties, and shrieking sixties provide ideal conditions for the ocean wanderers that can be encountered virtually anywhere in the vast southern ocean. Thus a species nesting on a tiny remote New Zealand Subantarctic island may routinely forage off the South American or African coast.

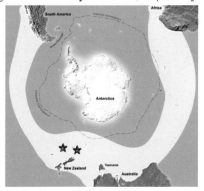

White-capped Albatross oceanic range

EMPEROR PENGUIN
Aptenodytes forsteri

44-90 lb (20-41kg): Largest penguin
Coastal Antarctica: Generally restricted to fast & pack-ice
- Large, oval-shaped pale yellow neck patches, variably tinged orange
- Proportionally short, partially feathered, decurved bill
- Fledges at about 45% of adult size
- Yearling nearly adult size, but w/ pale throat & neck patches

Juvenile

Chicks

Yearling

King Penguin
Aptenodytes patagonicus

21-38 lb (9.5-17.3kg): Second largest penguin
- Less robust than Emperor, w/ longer unfeathered bill
  - Bright orange, spoon-shaped ear patches
    - Smaller, paler juvenile may have black bill
      - Rookeries occupied year round

A. p. patagonicus
S Georgia, Falkland & possibly S Sandwich Is

Juvenile

Chick

A. p. halli
P Edward, Marion, Crozet, Kerguelen, Macquarie & Heard Is

- Virtually identical to *patagonicus*; subspecific status questionable

05

ADÉLIE PENGUIN
Pygoscelis adeliae

8.3-15.0 lb (3.8-6.8kg)

Antarctica, S Shetland, S Orkney, S Sandwich, Bouvetøya, Peter 1 Øy & Ballleny Is

- Conspicuous white eye-ring, small erectile crest & bill mainly feathered
- Smaller juvenile more bluish, w/ white throat, & no white eye-ring

Juvenile

Yearling

CHINSTRAP PENGUIN
Pygoscelis antarcticus

7.0-11.7 lb (3.2-5.3kg)
Antarctic Peninsula, S Shetland, S Orkney, S Sandwich,
S Georgia, Bouvetøya, Peter 1 Øy & Balleny Is
- Diagnostic black stripe across white throat
- Unfeathered black bill
- Face & throat of smaller juvenile speckled dark gray

Juvenile

GENTOO PENGUIN
Pygoscelis papua

9.9-18.7 lb (4.5-8.5kg)
- Orange-red bill & white triangular patch above & behind eyes
- Smaller juvenile has paler throat & less defined white over eyes

Northern Gentoo Penguin
P. p. papua

S Georgia, Falkland, P Edward, Marion,
Crozet, Kerguelen, Macquarie & Heard Is
- Larger, w/ longer bill more orange than red

Southern Gentoo Penguin
P. p. ellsworthi

N Antarctic Peninsula, S Shetland,
S Orkney & S Sandwich Is
- Smaller than *papua*, w/ shorter
  bill, flippers & feet

Juvenile

07

ROCKHOPPER PENGUIN
Eudyptes chrysocome

4.4-9.5 lb (2.0-4.3kg): Smallest of the six crested penguins
- Yellow eyebrows splay out at back of head as projecting crest
- Dark red-brown bill & bright red eyes
- Smaller juvenile has reduced or absent crest, grayish throat, darker bill & dull brown eyes

Juvenile

S. America

Falkland Is

Short-crested Rockhopper Penguin
E. c. chrysocome
Falkland Is & Cape Horn Archipelago

Eastern Rockhopper Penguin
E. c. filholi
P Edward, Marion, Crozet, Kerguelen, Macquarie, Heard, Auckland, Campbell, Antipodes & Bounty Is
- Narrow pinkish-flesh (not black) margin at bill base

Macquarie Is

Marion Is

BS

GT

Campbell Is

Eastern Rockhopper Penguin
E. c. filholi

Heard Is

Antipodes Is

JLK

BL

Crozet Is

Kerguelen Is

Long-crested Rockhopper Penguin
E. c. moseleyi

Tristan da Cunha, Gough,
Amsterdam & St Paul Is

- Very pronounced flowing,
  drooping yellow crest
- Slightly larger than *chrysocome*,
  w/ darker underflipper pattern
- Sometimes regarded as full species

MACARONI PENGUIN
Eudyptes chrysolophus

6.8-14.6 lb (3.1-6.6kg)

S Chilean Is, P Edward, Marion, Crozet, Kerguelen, Macquarie, Heard, Bouvetøya, S Georgia, Falkland, S Sandwich, S Orkney, S Shetland Is & N Antarctic Peninsula

• Golden-yellow crest joins across forehead
• Black throat & deep-based reddish-brown bill
• Conspicuous bare pink skin at bill base & gape

Juvenile

ROYAL PENGUIN
Eudyptes schlegeli

6.6-17.9 lb (3.0-8.1kg)

Macquarie Is

• Golden-yellow crest joins on forehead
• White throat; sometimes regarded as white-throated race of Macaroni Penguin
• Massive, deep-based reddish-brown bill
• Conspicuous bare pink skin at bill base & gape

Juvenile

SNARES PENGUIN
Eudyptes robustus
5.3-9.5 lb (2.4-4.4kg)
Snares Is
- Yellow stripe from bill base forms slightly bushy crest
- Bare pink skin at bill base & gape
- Smaller, duller juvenile has slight or absent crest

Juvenile

Chick

DOC

ERECT-CRESTED PENGUIN
Eudyptes sclateri
7.3-15.1 lb (3.3-7.0kg)
Bounty & Antipodes Is
- Erect, bush-like crest above & behind eye
- Reddish-brown bill
- Whitish line of bare skin around bill base
- Smaller, duller juvenile has slight or absent crest

JLK

Juvenile

FIORDLAND PENGUIN
Eudyptes pachyrhychus
4.6-11 lb (2.1-5.1kg)
SW New Zealand & offshore Is

- 3-6 white cheek stripes
- Yellow crest seldom appears bushy
- Large orange-red bill lacks bare pink skin at base & gape
- Rainforest species on 'mainland'; perhaps <2000 pairs

Juvenile

YELLOW-EYED PENGUIN
Megadyptes antipodes
8.0-19.6 lb (3.6-8.9kg)
Southern NZ, Auckland & Campbell Is

- Pale yellow eye
- Rather long, nearly straight, flesh-colored bill w/ red-brown tip
- Lemon-yellow band extends through eye & around hindcrown
- Juvenile has less conspicuous yellow head band
- Most threatened penguin; possibly <2000 pairs

Juvenile

Chick

12

MAGELLANIC PENGUIN
Spheniscus magellanicus

5.0-17.2 lb (2.3-7.8kg)
S Chile & Argentina: Falkland Is
- Double breast bands
- Breeding birds have bare pink skin around eye & bill base
- Smaller juvenile lacks head pattern & breast bands

Juvenile

Chick

AFRICAN (BLACK-FOOTED) PENGUIN
Spheniscus demersus

4.6-8.2 lb (2.1-3.7kg)
Southern Africa
- Single black chest band
- Smaller juvenile lacks head pattern & breast band

Juvenile

Chick

HUMBOLDT PENGUIN
Spheniscus humboltdi
7.9-12.8 lb (3.4-5.8kg)
Peru & Chile
- Larger bill, w/ more pink at base than Magellanic Penguin
- Single black band across upper chest
- Smaller juvenile lacks head pattern & breast band

Juvenile

GALAPAGOS PENGUIN
Spheniscus mendiculus
3.8-7.7lb (1.7-3.5kg)
Galapagos Islands (Ecuador)
- Double breast bands
- Facial markings rather indistinct

LITTLE (BLUE) PENGUIN
Eudyptula minor
1.1-4.6 lb (0.5-2.1kg): Smallest penguin
Australia & New Zealand
- Almost uniform metallic gray-blue dorsally
- Whitish-gray eyes
- Smaller juvenile often has bluer upperparts
- Nocturnal

Cook Strait Little Penguin
E. m. variabilis
S North Is & Cook Strait

14

LITTLE (BLUE) PENGUIN
Eudyptula minor

Northern Little Penguin
E. m. iredalei
Northern North Is

Chick

Australian Little Penguin
E. m. novaehollandiae
S Australia & Tasmania

Southern Little Penguin
E. m. minor
Western & SE South Is, & Stewart Is

Chatham Little Penguin
E. m. chathamensis
Chatham Is

White-flippered Little Penguin
E. m. albosignata
Banks Peninsula, E South Is
Chick
- White border on both leading & trailing edges of upper flipper
- Sometimes regarded as full species

WANDERING ALBATROSS
Diomedea exulans
14-25 lb (6.4-11.3kg); wingspan 8.2-11.5' (2.5-3.5m)

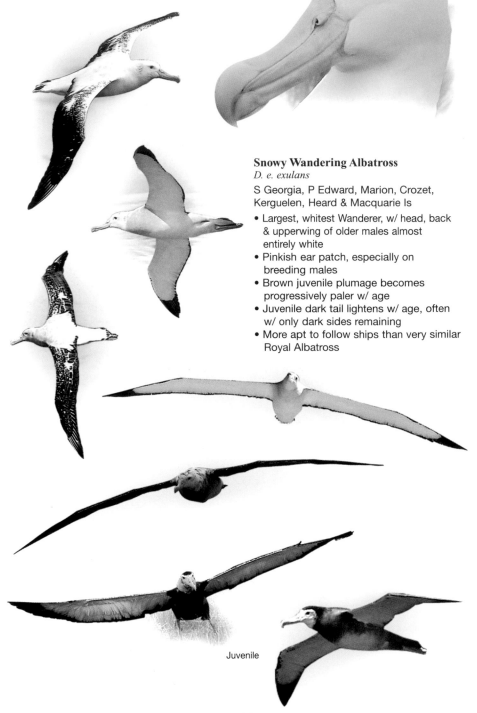

Snowy Wandering Albatross
D. e. exulans

S Georgia, P Edward, Marion, Crozet, Kerguelen, Heard & Macquarie Is

- Largest, whitest Wanderer, w/ head, back & upperwing of older males almost entirely white
- Pinkish ear patch, especially on breeding males
- Brown juvenile plumage becomes progressively paler w/ age
- Juvenile dark tail lightens w/ age, often w/ only dark sides remaining
- More apt to follow ships than very similar Royal Albatross

Juvenile

Juvenile

Gibson's Wandering Albatross
D. e. gibsoni

Auckland Is

- Upperwing mostly black, w/ white limited to 'elbow' region
- Female has more extensive dark cap than older male
- Immature may be nearly entirely brown, w/ white face mask

Juvenile

TP

JLK

Antipodean Wandering Albatross
D. e. antipodensis

Antipodes Is, w/ few on Campbell Is

- Darkest Wanderer
- Dimorphic: Female mostly brown, w/ white face
- Older male may have mottled brown crown patch & brown smudge on chest

♂

♂

♂

AC

JLK

AC

Tristan Wandering Albatross
D. e. dabbenena

Gough Is & formerly Tristan da Cunha

- Adult male not as white as Snowy Wanderer
- Dimorphic: Extensively vermiculated female irregularly blotched dusky, especially on sides. Older, mostly white female retains solid dark upperwing

♀

PR

♀

PR

PR

♂

PR

PR

18

ROYAL ALBATROSS
Diomedea epomophora

14.4-22.7 lb (6.5-10.3kg); wingspan 9.5-11.5' (2.9-3.5m)
- Both races lack dark juvenile stage
- Black cutting edge to upper mandible
- Lacks pinkish ear patch of most breeding Snowy Wanderers
- Mainly white tail, but juvenile has narrow, black terminal band

Southern Royal Albatross
D. e. epomophora

Campbell & Auckland Is
- Upperwing whiter than *sanfordi*, w/ black primaries, but some blackish barring projects 'dusty' appearance
- White leading edge of wing
- Juvenile upperwing mainly dark, progressively becoming white from leading edge backwards

Northern Royal Albatross
D. e. sanfordi

Chatham, w/ few in Auckland Is & Otago Peninsula, NZ
- Smaller than *epomophora*, w/ narrower wings
- Entire upperwing mostly solid black throughout life
- Diagnostic black leading edge from bend of underwing to tip
- Fledges w/ some dark speckling on crown & across lower back

CR

Juvenile

PH

PM/DOC

AW

AMSTERDAM ALBATROSS
Diomedea amsterdamensis

11.0-13.2 lb (5.0-6.0kg)

Amsterdam Is
- Large pink bill, w/ dark cutting edge on upper mandible & dusky tip
- Dark juvenile-type plumage retained for life
- Maximum 15 breeding pairs (1990); total population about 120 birds

PH

BL

CAB

WHITE-CAPPED ALBATROSS
Thalassarche cauta
7.1-11.2 lb (3.2-5.1kg); wingspan 6.8-8.5' (210-260cm)
- Along w/ Salvin's & Chatham Albatrosses, the largest mollymawk, w/ stoutest bill
- Narrow black underwing margin, w/ diagnostic black 'thumb mark' at base of leading edge

CR

DH

DH

White-capped Albatross
T. c. steadi
Auckland & Antipodes Is
- Head white, w/ variable grayish smudging over cheek & ear area
- Prominent black eye-patch
- Virtually identical to Shy Albatross, but slightly larger, w/ duller gray bill

GT/DOC

CR

GT

TP

Shy (Tasmanian) Albatross
T. c. cauta
Mewston, Pedra Branca & Albatross Is, Tasmania
- Practically inseparable from *steadi*, but paler white-gray bill more yellowish, w/ yellow tip

SALVIN'S ALBATROSS
Thalassarche salvini

7.3-10.8 lb (3.3-4.9kg); wingspan 6.8-8.5' (210-260cm)

Bounty & Snares Is, w/ few pairs at Crozet Is

- Medium-gray head & neck contrasts w/ white forehead
- Bluish-gray bill has ivory-horn or yellowish top & black tip
- Narrow black underwing margin, w/ black 'thumb mark' at base of leading edge

TP

CR

CHATHAM ALBATROSS
Thalassarche eremita

6.8-10.4 lb (3.1-4.7kg); wingspan 6.8-8.5' (210-260cm)

Pyramid Rock: Chatham Is

- Dark gray head & neck contrasts w/ white underparts
- Bright yellow bill w/ dark tip on lower mandible
- Narrow black underwing margin, w/ broad, black tip & black 'thumb mark' at base of leading edge

CR

CR

22

BLACK-BROWED ALBATROSS
Thalassarche melanophris

6.4-10.0 lb (2.6-4.6kg); wingspan 6.9-8.2' (210-250cm)
- Prominent black eyebrows
- Black leading underwing margin widest of any albatross
- Mainly white-headed juvenile sometimes has gray collar, w/ small ill-defined eye patch. Unlike similar Gray-headed Albatross juvenile, has grayish or horn-colored (not black) bill w/ black tip

Black-browed Albatross
T. m. melanophris

S Chile, S Georgia, Falkland, Crozet, Kerguelen, Campbell, Macquarie, Heard, Snares & Antipodes Is
- Dark colored eye
- Bright orange-yellow bill w/ reddish tip

Juvenile

Campbell Black-browed Albatross
T. m. impavida

Campbell Is
- Pale honey-colored eye, w/ bill tip more orange than red
- Black eyebrow more extensive, w/ slightly darker underwing

DOC

PJM

GRAY-HEADED ALBATROSS
Thalassarche chrysostoma
5.7-9.7 lb (2.6-4.4kg); wingspan 7.2' (220cm)
S South Amer Is, S Georgia, P Edward, Marion,
Kerguelen, Macquarie & Campbell Is
- Medium to dark gray head, w/ pale forehead
- Narrow yellow stripe on top & bottom of orange-tipped, glossy black bill
- Similar to Buller's & smaller, more slender Yellow-nosed Albatrosses, but darker
  underwing has broader black trailing edge margin
- Black-billed juvenile underwing may appear
  uniform black

BH

AB

Juvenile

AS

24

BULLER'S ALBATROSS
Thalassarche bulleri

4.6-7.5 lb (2.1-3.4kg); wingspan 6.7-7.0' (200-213cm)
- Black bill, w/ broad, bright yellow stripe on both mandibles
- Thick, black margin on underwing leading edge, w/ very thin trailing edge margin
- Unlike similar Gray-headed Albatross, has contrasting white forehead

AP

Southern Buller's Albatross
T. b. bulleri

Snares & Solander (NZ) Is
- Gray head, w/ silvery-white forehead patch
- Yellow on bill slightly broader than *platei*

GP/DOC

AB

GP/DOC

RM

Northern (Pacific) Buller's Albatross
T. b. platei

Chatham Is
- Very similar to *bulleri*, but has wider bill
- Darker gray head, w/ smaller, more contrasting whitish forecrown

CR

CR

25

YELLOW-NOSED ALBATROSS
Thalassarche chlororhynchos

4.1-6.2 lb (1.9-2.8kg); wingspan 5.9-6.6' (180-200cm)
- Smallest, most slender albatross
- Yellow confined to top ridge of long, thin, glossy black bill, w/ pinkish tip

Eastern (Indian) Yellow-nosed Albatross
T. c. bassi

Amsterdam, St Paul, P Edward, Marion, Crozet & Kerguelen Is
- Mostly white head, w/ gray confined to face
- Yellow atop bill pointed at bill base, rather than more rounded as in *chlororhynchos*

BL

Western (Atlantic) Yellow-nosed Albatross
T. c. chlororhynchos

Tristan da Cunha & Gough Is
- Head & neck more extensively gray than *bassi*

BH

Fledgling

BH

PR

26

Light-mantled Sooty Albatross
Phoebetria palpebrata

5.5-8.2 lb (2.5-3.7kg); wingspan 5.9-7.2' (180-220cm)

S Georgia, P Edward, Marion, Crozet, Kerguelen, Heard, Macquarie, Auckland, Campbell & Antipodes Is

- Ashy-gray upperparts
- Long, narrow wings
- Pale bluish stripe on lower mandible of black bill
- Partial white eye-ring
- Long pointed tail
- Most likely albatross to reach southern ice

SOOTY ALBATROSS
Phoebetria fusca

4.0-6.6 lb (1.8-3.0kg); wingspan 6.7' (203cm)

Tristan da Cunha, P Edward, Marion, Kerguelen, Amsterdam & St Paul Is

- Uniformly dark upperparts
- Long, narrow wings & long, pointed tail
- Yellow or cream stripe on lower mandible of black bill
- Partial white eye-ring

FJ

CAB

PR

BL

NORTHERN GIANT-PETREL
Macronectes halli

8.4-11.0 lb (3.8-5.0kg); wingspan 4.9-6.9' (150-210cm)

S Georgia, P Edward, Marion, Crozet, Kerguelen, Macquarie, Auckland, Campbell, Antipodes, Chatham & Stewart Is

- Albatross size, but appears hump-backed in flight
- Prominent tubes atop huge bill w/ reddish tip
- Dark juvenile becomes paler w/ age
- Both giant-petrel species are powerful
  scavengers & predators

SOUTHERN GIANT-PETREL
Macronectes giganteus

8.4-11.0 lb (3.8-5.0kg); wingspan 4.9-6.9' (150-210cm)

S Chile, Falkland, S Georgia, S Sandwich, S Orkney, S Shetland, P Edward, Marion, Crozet, Kerguelen, Heard & Macquarie Is; Antarctic Peninsula & E Antarctica

- Albatross size, but in flight appears hump-backed
- Prominent nasal tubes atop huge bill w/ pale greenish tip
- Dark juvenile becomes progressively lighter w/ age
- White morph
- When feeding on carcass, head & neck may be red

SOUTHERN (ANTARCTIC) FULMAR
Fulmarus glacialoides

1.5-2.2 lb (0.7-1.0kg); wingspan 3.7'-3.9' (114-120cm)

Antarctica: Peter 1 Øy, Bouvetøya, S Sandwich, S Orkney & S Shetland Is

• Pale bluish-gray, gull-like plumage
• Conspicuous white wing-patch
• Pinkish bill w/ black tip
• Pinkish legs & feet

ANTARCTIC PETREL
Thalassoica antarctica

24 oz (657g); wingspan 3.2-3.6' (100-110cm)

Coastal Antarctica to 217 mi (350km) inland

• Head, neck, back & rump dark brown
• White trailing edge to upper wing
• Dark brown terminal band on white tail
• Normally associated w/ pack-ice

CAPE (PAINTED) PETREL
Daption capense

15.5 oz (440g); wingspan 2.6-2.9' (80-91cm)
- Boldly checkered upperparts
- Habitual ship follower

Cape Petrel (Cape Pigeon)
D. c. capense
Antarctica: Peter 1 Øy, S Georgia, S Sandwich, S Orkney, S Shetland, Crozet, Kerguelen, Heard, Bouvetøya & Macquarie Is

New Zealand (Snares) Cape Petrel
D. c. australe
Chatham, Snares, Auckland, Campbell, Antipodes & Bounty Is
- Smaller & darker, w/ smaller white upperwing patches

SNOW PETREL
Pagodroma nivea

7-20 oz (200-570g); wingspan 2.5-3.1' (75-95cm)
- Entirely white except for black bill, eyes & feet
- Relatively long wings & mostly squarish tail
- May appear dark due to sea reflection
- Normally associated w/ pack-ice

Lesser Snow Petrel
P. n. nivea
S Georgia, S Sandwich, S Orkney, S Shetland Is, & coastal Antarctica to 214 mi (345km) inland

Greater Snow Petrel
P. n. confusa
- Larger, w/ broader wings & thicker bill
- Great overlap in size & range, w/ 'pure' colonies known only from Balleny Is

WHITE-HEADED PETREL
Pterodroma lessonii

20.5-28.6 oz (580-810g); wingspan 3.6' (109cm)

Crozet, Kerguelen, Macquarie, Auckland, Antipodes Is, & possibly Campbell, P Edward & Marion Is

- Large, robust gadfly petrel, w/ deep-based black bill
- Conspicuous black eye patch
- Only petrel w/ whitish head, rump & tail
- Partial gray collar
- Upperparts & underwing uniformly grayish-black
- Round-tipped tail slightly wedge-shaped
- Proportionally long wings
- May be attracted to ships, but seldom follows

AB

FG

RP

RP

32

Mottled (Scaled) Petrel
Pterodroma inexpectata
11.1 oz (315g); wingspan 2.8' (85cm)
Snares Is & islets off Stewart Is, NZ
- Robust gadfly petrel, w/ mottled frosty-gray upperparts
- White underwing, w/ bold, black, crescent-shaped mark extending inward from bend of wing
- Blackish M-mark across upperwings
- Dark gray patch on white belly

PH

DM

WC

Fledgling

PH

Atlantic (Schlegel's) Petrel
Pterodroma incerta
18.3 oz (520g); wingspan 3.4' (104cm)
Tristan da Cunha & Gough Is
- Large, robust gadfly petrel
- Dark head, underwing, upper breast, vent & tail contrast w/ white belly
- Uniformly dark brown upperparts
- Deep-based black bill
- Slightly wedge-shaped tail

PH

BH

PH

PH

SOFT-PLUMAGED PETREL
Pterodroma mollis

9.8-11.0 oz (279-312g); wingspan 2.7-3.1' (83-95cm)

Tasmania, Marion, Crozet, Kerguelen, Antipodes, Tristan da Cunha & Gough Is

- Ashy-gray upperparts, w/ faint M mark across wings & back
- Black bill, white chin & throat, & dark oval eye-patch
- Dark smudges on sides of breast may form broad complete breast band
- Rather rare melanistic morph described, but possibly is
  a hybrid w/ Kerguelen Petrel

GREAT-WINGED PETREL
Pterodroma macroptera

16-22 oz (460-750g); wingspan 3.2-3.3' (97-102cm)

Offshore NZ Is, Tristan da Cunha, Gough, Marion, Crozet,
Kerguelen & Amsterdam Is

- Overall blackish-brown
- Dark underwing
- Rather long, slightly wedge-shaped tail
- Stocky body & rounded head
- Large, deep-based black bill
- Varying pale face & forehead

KERGUELEN PETREL
Aphrodroma (Pterodroma) brevirostris

12.3 oz (357g); wingspan 2.6-2.7' (80-82cm)

Marion, Crozet, Kerguelen, Gough Is, & probably Tristan da Cunha

- Proportionally large head, w/ high, steep forehead
- Short, stubby black bill
- Dark slate-gray plumage appears silvery in sunlight, especially underwing
- Face often appears darker

GRAY PETREL
Procellaria cinerea

1.7-3.3 lb (0.76-1.5kg); wingspan 3.8-4.3' (115-130cm)

Tristan da Cunha, Gough, Marion, Crozet, Kerguelen, Campbell, Antipodes & possibly St Paul Is (Formerly Macquarie Is)

- Robust, heavy-bodied petrel
- Slender greenish-yellow bill
- Uniform ashy-gray dorsally, w/ darkish crown & face
- White underparts contrast w/ dark underwing
- Short, gray wedge-shaped tail

WHITE-CHINNED PETREL
Procellaria aequinoctialis

2.2-3.0 lb (1.0-1.4kg); wingspan 4.3-4.8' (134-147cm)
- Large, uniformly blackish-brown petrel
- Bulbous pale ivory-yellow bill very evident from afar

White-chinned Petrel
P. a. aequinoctialis

Falkland, S Georgia, P Edward, Marion, Crozet, Kerguelen, Auckland, Campbell & Antipodes Is

- White chin seldom discernable at sea
- May be partially leucistic

Tristan White-chinned (Spectacled) Petrel
P. a. conspicillata

Tristan da Cunha

- White may encircle cheeks giving 'spectacled' appearance
- Often regarded as full species

GREATER SHEARWATER
Puffinus gravis
1.6-2.0 lb (715-959g); wingspan 3.3-3.0' (100-118cm)
Falkland, Tristan da Cunha & Gough Is
- Dusky grayish-brown dorsally
- Dark brown cap & white hind-collar
- Pale-edged dark feathers on back & upperwings project scaled appearance

BH

PR

FLESH-FOOTED SHEARWATER
Puffinus carneipes
NZ & offshore Is: St Paul Is
1.2-1.6 lb (533-730g); wingspan 3.2-3.5' (99-107cm)
- Large, wholly blackish-brown petrel, w/ dark underwing
- Yellowish-pink or flesh-colored bill w/ black tip
- Distinctive flesh-colored legs

TP

AS

LITTLE SHEARWATER
Puffinus assimilis
7.8-9.2 oz (220-260g); wingspan 1.9-2.2' (58-67cm)
NZ offshore Is: Chatham, Antipodes, St Paul, Tristan da Cunha & Gough Is
- Smallest shearwater, w/ rather small bill
- Bill black along top & pale blue on sides
- Black upperparts & white underparts
- Distinctive white face & black cap

BH

TG

SOOTY SHEARWATER
Puffinus griseus

1.4-2.1 lb (650-950g); wingspan 3.0-3.4' (94-105cm)

NZ & S South Amer Is, Tasmania: Tristan da Cunha, Falkland, Macquarie, Chatham, Snares, Auckland, Campbell & Antipodes Is

- Mostly sooty chocolate-brown
- Silvery underwings
- Larger & darker, w/ more sloping forehead & longer bill than similar Short-tailed Shearwater

PJM

RM

DV

SHORT-TAILED SHEARWATER
Puffinus tenuirostris

1.0-1.8 lb (480-800g); wingspan 3.1-3.3' (95-100cm)

Tasmania

- Mainly sooty-brown overall
- Shorter bill than larger, darker Sooty Shearwater, w/ steeper forehead
- Grayer, rather than silvery underwing

DH

RP

ANTARCTIC (DOVE) PRION
Pachyptila desolata

3.4-7.9 oz (95-224g); wingspan 22.0-30.0" (58-66cm)

S Georgia, S Sandwich, S Orkney, S Shetland, Crozet,
Kerguelen, Heard, Macquarie & Auckland Is, & formerly Antarctica
- Blue-gray like all prions, w/ dark M across upper wing
- Stout, broad bluish bill, w/ lamellae normally not visible at base
- Identical to Salvin's Prion, but bill slightly shorter & narrower
- Fast, erratic & bouyant flight

MH

SALVIN'S PRION
Pachyptila salvini

4.9-7.4 oz (130-210g); wingspan 22.4" (57cm)

P Edward, Marion & Crozet Is
- Inseparable from *P. desolata* at sea, but has purer white face & less gray on breast & sides
- Lamellae visible at base of slightly longer, broader bluish bill

    St Paul Prion *(P. macgillivrayi)* often regarded as race of Salvin's Prion
    (not illustrated); total population merely 150-200 pairs

MH

AB

AB

BROAD-BILLED PRION
Pachyptila vittata

6.0-8.4 oz (170-237g)
Wingspan 22.4-30.0" (57-66cm)

NZ & offshore Is: Chatham, Snares,
Tristan da Cunha & Gough Is

- Broad black tip to tail
- Very large head, w/ high forehead
- Darkish head, w/ distinct white eyebrow
- Largest prion, w/ massive black (not blue) bill

PH

SLENDER-BILLED PRION
Pachyptila belcheri

4.1-6.3 oz (115-180g); wingspan 22" (56cm)

S Chilean Is, Falkland, Crozet & Kerguelen Is

- Slender bluish bill
- Black in tail reduced to small central spot
- Paler face, w/ more evident white eyebrow than any prion
- Upperparts paler, w/ less distinct dorsal black M than
  any prion

MH

TC

40

FULMAR PRION
Pachyptila crassirostris

3.4-6.5 oz (102-185g); wingspan 23.7" (60cm)

Heard, Snares, Auckland, Bounty & Chatham Is

- Paler blue-gray than similar Fairy Prion, w/ more distinct dorsal M & slightly stouter bill
- Broad, black tail tip
- Indistinct facial pattern

FAIRY PRION
Pachyptila turtur

3.1-6.2 oz (88-175g); wingspan 22.0-23.7" (56-60cm)

NZ & offshore Is & Tasmania: Chatham, Snares, Antipodes, Macquarie, Kerguelen, St Paul, Crozet, Marion, S Georgia & Falkland Is

- Smallest prion, w/ broad, black tail band
- Very pale head, w/ indistinct grayish eye stripe, lacking blackish line behind eye
- Inseparable from Fulmar Prion at sea, but has shorter, paler, thinner blue bill

41

BLUE PETREL
Halobaena caerulea

5.5-8.6 oz (152-251g); wingspan 2.0-2.3' (62-71cm)

S South Amer Is, S Georgia, P Edward, Marion, Crozet, Kerguelen & Macquarie Is

- Resembles a prion, but square (not wedge shaped) tail broadly tipped white, not black
- Black cap extends to sides of breast forming collar
- Darker head, w/ large white forehead patch
- Narrower blackish (not blue) bill

MH

TC

MH

MH

WILSON'S STORM-PETREL
Oceanites oceanicus

1.0-1.8 oz (28-50g); wingspan 15.0-16.5" (38-42cm)

S Chilean Is, Falkland, S Georgia, S Sandwich, S Orkney, S Shetland, Bouvetøya, P Edward, Marion, Crozet, Kerguelen, Macquarie, Peter 1 Øy & Heard Is, & Antarctica

- Very dark brown above & below, w/ prominent white rump
- Only southern storm-petrel w/ completely black belly
- Pale upperwing bar on rounded wing
- Yellow foot webs
- Feet extend beyond square tail

GRAY-BACKED STORM-PETREL
Oceanites nereis

0.7-1.6 oz (21-44g); wingspan 15.4" (39cm)

Falkland, S Georgia, P Edward, Marion, Gough,
Crozet, Kerguelen & Auckland Is
- Blackish-gray upperparts may become
  browner w/ wear
- Blackish head, w/ pale gray rump & upper tail
- White underparts & square, dark-tipped tail

WHITE-FACED STORM-PETREL
Oceanites marina

1.4-2.5 oz (40-70g); wingspan 17" (43 cm)

Tasmania & NZ: Chatham, Auckland Is & Tristan da Cunha
- Large gray-brown storm-petrel
- White face & eyebrow, gray crown & dark eye-stripe
- Pale upperwing bar & gray rump
- Yellow-webbed feet project beyond
  slightly forked tail

WHITE-BELLIED STORM-PETREL
Fregetta grallaria
1.6-2.6 oz (45-74g); wingspan 18.9" (48cm)
P Edward, St Paul, Tristan da Cunha & Gough Is
- Pure white belly & white rump
- Not as dark as smaller Black-bellied Storm-Petrel
- Upperparts project scaled appearance
- Feet only marginally project beyond square tail

PH

PH

TL

BLACK-BELLIED STORM-PETREL
Oceanites tropica
1.5-2.2 oz (43-63g); wingspan 18" (46cm)
P Edward, Crozet, Kerguelen, Auckland, Antipodes, Bounty, Bouvetøya, S Georgia, S Orkney & S Shetland Is
- Robust, blackish-brown petrel, w/ white rump
- Black line down center of white belly often difficult to see
- Broad dark margin on white underwing

FJ

RP

AB

COMMON DIVING-PETREL
Pelecanoides urinatrix

3.0-6.5 oz (86-185g): wingspan 13-15" (33-38cm)

Tasmania & NZ: Falkland, S Georgia, Tristan da Cunha, Gough, Marion, Crozet, Kerguelen, Heard, Macquarie, Chatham, Snares, Auckland, Campbell & Antipodes Is

- Larger & stockier than *P. georgicus,* but inseparable at sea
- Underwings & belly more grayish
- Cobalt-blue legs of adult lack black line extending down back
- Longer, narrower bill has parallel-sided base that tapers toward tip

SOUTH GEORGIAN DIVING-PETREL
Pelecanoides georgicus

3.2-5.3 oz (90-150g); wingspan 12-13" (30-33cm)

S Georgia, P Edward, Marion, Crozet, Kerguelen, Heard, Auckland & Codfish (NZ) Is

- Basically inseparable from *P. urinatrix,* but w/ whitish, not gray, underwing
- Blacker upper wing, w/ white trailing edge
- Cobalt-blue legs have black line down back
- Shorter, broader bill, w/ more tapering sides & different nostril configuration

ANTARCTIC (BLUE-EYED) SHAG
Phalacrocorax bransfieldensis
5.5-6.6 lb (2.5-3.0kg)
N Antarctic Peninsula, S Shetland & Elephant Is
- Extensive white cheeks
- Prominent white upper back

Juvenile

HEARD SHAG
Phalacrocorax nivalis
6.1-7.3 lb (2.8-3.3kg)
Heard Is
- Extensive white shoulders
  may be absent

BW

CROZET SHAG
Phalacrocorax melanogenis
4.0-5.1 lb (1.8-2.3kg)
Crozet, P Edward & Marion Is
- Black head & cheeks
- Limited white on shoulders
- Upper back lacks white patch

CAB

46

MACQUARIE SHAG
Phalacrocorax purpurascens
4.9-7.7 lb (2.2-3.5kg)
Macquarie Is
- White restricted to lower cheeks
- Normally lacks white on upper back
- White on shoulders not extensive

Chick

KERGUELEN SHAG
Phalacrocorax verrucosus
3.3-4.9 lb (1.5-2.2kg)
Kerguelen Is
- Smallest & overall darkest of 'blue-eyed' complex
- Black face
- Limited or no white on shoulders
- No white patch on upper back

SOUTH GEORGIAN SHAG
Phalacrocorax georgianus
5.5-6.4 lb (2.5-6.4kg)
S Georgia, S Orkney & S Sandwich Is
- White on back less extensive than Antarctic Shag
- Demarcation between black & white on face at eye level

AUCKLAND SHAG
Phalacrocorax colensoi
4.4 lb (2.0kg)
Auckland Is
- Foreneck pure white or w/ extensive black nearly meeting in front
- Bare maroon facial skin

CAMPBELL SHAG
Phalacrocorax campbelli
3.5-4.4 lb (1.6-2.0kg)
Campbell Is
- Black neck, w/ white throat
- Bare dusky-purple facial skin

BOUNTY SHAG
Phalacrocorax ranfurlyi
5.0-6.4 lb (2.3-2.9kg)
Bounty Is
- Bare reddish facial skin
- Possibly <1200 shags

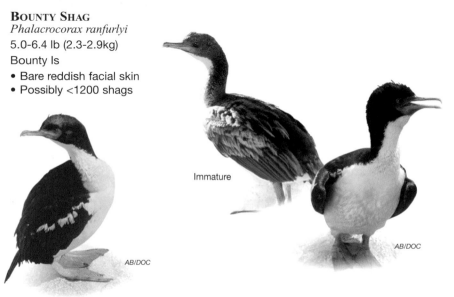

Immature

AB/DOC

AB/DOC

48

AUSTRALIAN SHELDUCK
Tadorna tadornoides
2.8-3.4 lbs (1.3-1.5kg)
Nested Campbell Is mid-1980s; vagrant
to Auckland & Macquarie Is

PACIFIC BLACK DUCK
Anas superciliosa
1.3-3.1 lb (0.6-1.4kg)
Aust & NZ: Chatham, Snares, Auckland, Campbell & Macquarie Is
• Speculum glossy greenish, not bluish

AUCKLAND MERGANSER †
Mergus australis
2.0 lb (0.9kg)
• Discovered 1840 & extinct by 1902

SPECKLED (YELLOW-BILLED) TEAL
Anas f. flavirostris
14-15 oz (394-429g)
S Amer: Falkland & S Georgia Is
• <100 teal at S Georgia Is

AUCKLAND TEAL
Anas aucklandica

0.8-1.7 lb (375-621g)

Auckland Is

- Flightless
- Sexes similar, but greenish cast reduced or lacking in female
- Population about 2,500 ducks

♂

♂

CAMPBELL TEAL
Anas nesiotis

11.1-17.6 oz (315-500g)

- Flightless
- Smaller & darker than very similar Auckland Teal
- Among rarest of birds, w/ merely 30-100 teal on rat-free Dent Is
- Campbell Is designated rat free in 2003; teal to be reintroduced

♂

♀

EATON'S PINTAIL
Anas eatoni
0.9-1.2 lb (430-502g)
• Population <10,000 ducks

FJ

Kerguelen Pintail
A. e. eatoni

FJ

FJ

♂

Crozet Pintail
A. e. drygalskii
• Slightly smaller than *eatoni*,
  w/ shorter wings & longer legs
• Somewhat paler, w/ more buff on breast

♂

CAD

SOUTH GEORGIA PINTAIL
Anas g. georgica
1.0-1.5 lb (460-660g)
S Georgia Is
• Smaller, darker & redder than
  South American race, w/ rounder
  head & shorter, more upturned
  brighter yellow bill
• Population estimated at
  about 1,000 prs

NEW ZEALAND FALCON
Falco novaeseelandiae
8.9-10.4 oz (252-294g)
NZ: Auckland Is, w/ possibly 10 pairs in 1990

INACCESSIBLE ISLAND RAIL
Atlantisia rogersi
1.2-1.7 oz (34-49g)
Inaccessible Island, Tristan da Cunha
• World's smallest flightless bird
• Population estimated at 8,400 rails

PR

AUCKLAND ISLAND RAIL
Dryolimnas muelleri
2.2-3.5 oz (63-100g)
Adams & Disappointment Is, Auckland Is
• Stable population estimated at
  about 2,000 rails

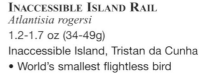

RM

GOUGH MOORHEN
Gallinula comeri
14.1-18.7 oz (400-530g)
Gough Is: introduced Tristan da Cunha 1956
• Practically flightless
• Increasing population between
  4,500 & 6,500 birds

PR

BLACK-FACED (LESSER) SHEATHBILL
Chionis minor
0.9-1.7 lb (450-760g); wingspan 2.4-2.6' (74-79cm)
P Edward, Marion, Kerguelen, Crozet & Heard Is
• Four races differ mainly in bill sheath shape & leg color
• Bare pinkish eye-ring
• Short, broad wings
• Walks w/ pigeon-like bobbing of head
• Fearless & extremely inquisitive

ES

Heard Sheathbill
C. m. nasicornis

Kerguelen Sheathbill
C. m. minor

Marion Sheathbill
C. m. marionensis

BS

Crozet Sheathbill
C. m. crozettensis

SNOWY (AMERICAN) SHEATHBILL
Chionis albus

1.0-1.7 lb (460-780g); wingspan 2.4-2.8' (74-84cm)

S Georgia, S Orkney, S Shetland Is & N Antarctic Peninsula

- Stout, yellowish-horn bill has horny sheath
- Only Antarctic-breeding bird lacking webbed feet
- Walks w/ pigeon-like bobbing of head
- Fearless & extremely inquisitive

AUCKLAND DOUBLE-BANDED PLOVER (DOTTEREL)
Charadrius bicinctus exilis

1.7-3.1 oz (47-89g)

Auckland Is; Enderby & Adams Is

- Population estimated at 730 plovers in 1989

AS

54

NEW ZEALAND SNIPE
Coenocorypha aucklandica
2.9-4.6 oz (82-131g)

Auckland Snipe
C. a. aucklandica
• Whitish underparts

GT

MW

Antipodes Snipe
C. a. meinertzhagenae
• Darkest race, w/ most
yellow on underparts

Snares Snipe
C. a. huegeli
• Completely barred underparts

RM

JC

Campbell Snipe
C. a. spp?
• Rediscovered on rat-free Jacquemart Is
(Campbell Is) in 1997, after not being seen
since 1964

Juvenile

RED-BILLED GULL
Larus scopulinus
8.6-12.7 oz (245-360g); wingspan 3.0-3.1' (91-96cm)
NZ: Chatham, Snares, Auckland & Campbell Is
• Conspicuous red bill & legs
• Silver-gray back & wings
• Juvenile has brown mottling on upper wings,
pinkish bill w/ dark tip, & dull pinkish legs

KELP (DOMINICAN) GULL
Larus dominicanus

2.0-3.0 lb (0.9-1.3 kg); wingspan 4.2-4.7' (128-142cm)

Antarctic Peninsula, S Shetland, S Orkney, S Sandwich, Bouvetøya, Falkland & all Subantarctic Is

- Only Antarctic gull
- Yellow bill w/ red spot on lower mandible
- Olive-yellow legs

Juvenile

AS

COMMON (BROWN) NODDY
Anous stolidus

5.3-9.6 oz (150-272g)
Wingspan 2.5-2.8' (75-86cm)

Mainly tropical, but south to Tristan da Cunha & Gough Is

- Overall dark brown w/ pale forehead & crown
- Broad tail w/ shallow fork

WHITE-FRONTED TERN
Sterna striata

3.6-5.6 oz (103-160g); wingspan 2.5-2.6' (79-82cm)

Tasmania & NZ: Chatham & Auckland Is

- White, w/ pale gray wings & prominent black cap
- Band of white between cap & black bill
- Moderately long, deeply forked tail

ANTARCTIC TERN
Sterna vittata

4.0-7.2 oz (114-205g); wingspan 2.4-2.6' (74-79cm)
Antarctic Peninsula & virtually all Subantarctic Is
- Red bill & feet
- Gray body & wings, & white rump
- Deeply forked tail

Juvenile

BH

ARCTIC TERN
Sterna paradisaea

3.0-4.5 oz (86-127g); wingspan 2.5-2.9' (76-85cm)
Arctic nester, but winters south to Antarctica
- Pale gray dorsally & white ventrally
- Deeply forked tail, w/ long streamers
- Similar to Antarctic Tern, but separable
  due to juvenile or non-breeding plumage

Juvenile

SOOTY TERN
Sterna fuscata

5.3-9.6 oz (150-272g); wingspan 2.5-2.8' (75-86cm)
Mainly tropical, but nested once St Paul Is
- Conspicuous black wings & cap
- White forehead & underparts
- Long, forked tail
- Black bill & legs

AS

KERGUELEN TERN
Sterna virgata

2.3-6.0 oz (85-170g); wingspan 2.2-2.4' (68-72cm)

Kerguelen, Crozet, P Edward & Marion Is

• Overall darker than Antarctic Tern, w/ shorter bill
• Gray (not white) upper & under tail
• Deep-red bill & orange to dull red legs

Non-breeding plumage

FJ

FJ

FJ

SOUTH POLAR SKUA
Stercorarius (Catharacta) maccormicki

1.3-3.7 lb (0.6-1.7 kg)

Wingspan 4.1-5.3' (126-160cm)

Antarctica north to S Shetland Is

• Smaller than Brown Skua, w/ shorter, stubbier bill
• Variable plumage from very pale to all dark
• Many have golden nape hackles
• Conspicuous wing white patch
• May hybridize w/ Brown Skua in Antarctic Peninsula region

Brown (Subantarctic) Skua
Stercorarius (Catharacta) antarcticus
2.8-6.0 lb (1.3-2.5kg); wingspan 4.1-5.3' (126-160cm)
Antarctic Peninsula, S Shetland, S Orkney,
S Sandwich, Falklands & all Subantarctic Is
- Uniform dark brown
- Bold white wing patches
- Larger & heavier than South Polar Skua

Brown (Subantarctic) Skua
S. a. lonnbergi

Tristan Brown Skua
S. a. hamiltoni
Tristan da Cunha & Gough Is
- Inseparable from *lonnbergi*, except when in range

PR

BH

59

ANTIPODES PARAKEET
Cyanoramphus unicolor
3.5-7.4 oz (99-219g)
Antipodes Is
• May feed on penguin carcasses & broken eggs
• May kill & feed on nesting petrels in holes
• Nests in burrows >1m deep at base
  of tussac grass
• Population estimated at between
  2,000 & 3,000 parakeets

RED-CROWNED PARAKEET
Cyanoramphus novaezelandiae
1.5-4.0 oz (43-113g)
NZ: Auckland & Antipodes Is (Extinct on
Macquarie Is)
• Commonly forages on ground
• Feeds on seeds, fruit, leaves, buds,
  nectar, invertebrates & even carrion

YELLOW-CROWNED PARAKEET
Cyanoramphus auriceps
1.3-1.9 oz (37-55g)
NZ: Auckland Is
• Common on main Auckland Is, but far outnumbered by
  larger Red-crowned Parakeet on other smaller islands
• Less likely to feed on ground
• Hybridizes w/ *C. novaezelandiae*

SOUTH GEORGIA PIPIT
Anthus antarcticus
S Georgia Is, where confined to a few rat-free 'mainland' sites & some 20 rat-free islets
• Population estimated at 3,000-4,000 prs

Campbell Is

NEW ZEALAND PIPIT
Anthus novaeseelandiae
1.4 oz (40g)
NZ: Chatham, Auckland, Campbell & Antipodes Is

Auckland Is

Pied morph

NEW ZEALAND FANTAIL
Rhipidura f. fuliginosa
1.1-1.4 oz (31-40g)
NZ: Snares Is

Juvenile

DC/DOC

RM

TRISTAN THRUSH
Nesocichla eremita
2.6-4.4 oz (76-124g)
Tristan da Cunha
• Population estimated at 6,000 birds in the 1980s

PR

BH

61

SNARES ISLAND FERNBIRD
Megalurus punctatus caudatus
1.1-1.4 oz (31-40g)
Snares Is
• Population estimated at
1,500 pairs

RM

TUI
Prosthemadera novaeseelandiae
3.9-5.3 oz (110-150g)
NZ: Chatham & Auckland Is

AS

AUCKLAND ISLAND TOMTIT
Petroica macrocephala marrineri
0.4 oz (11g)
Auckland Is

SNARES ISLAND TOMTIT
Petroica macrocephala dannefaerdi
0.6-0.8 oz (18-23g)
Snares Is
• Estimated 500 birds in 1987

♂

RA

NEW ZEALAND BELLBIRD
Anthornis m. melanura
0.9-1.2 oz (26-34g)
NZ: Auckland Is

GRAY-BACKED SILVEREYE
Zosterops l. lateralis
0.4-0.6 oz (10.1-16.5g)
Aust & NZ: Chatham, Snares,
Auckland, Campbell &
Antipodes Is

CSK

PR/DOC

GOUGH BUNTING
Rowettia goughensis
Gough Is
• Population estimated at
1,500 prs in 1991

PR

TRISTAN BUNTING
Nesospiza acunhae
0.8-1.2 oz (24-34g)
Tristan da Cunha
• Population estimated
at about 30,000 birds

BH

PR

GROSBEAK BUNTING
Nesospiza wilkinsi
1.4-1.6 oz (41-45g)
Nightingale & Inaccessible Is,
Tristan da Cunha
• Estimated only 500 pure birds;
hybridizes w/ Tristan Bunting

PR

INTRODUCED NEW ZEALAND EXOTICS

MALLARD
Anas platyrhynchos
Snares, Auckland, Campbell,
Antipodes & Macquarie Is

♂

♀

♀

COMMON (EUROPEAN) BLACKBIRD
Turdus merula
Snares, Auckland, Campbell & Antipodes Is

♂

SONG THRUSH
Turdus philomelos
Snares, Auckland, Campbell & Antipodes Is

COMMON REDPOLL
Carduelis flammea
Snares, Auckland, Campbell,
Antipodes & Macquarie Is

DV

♂

RM

YELLOWHAMMER
Emberiza citrinella
Snares & Campbell Is

MFS

COMMON STARLING
Sturnus vulgaris
Snares, Auckland, Campbell,
Antipodes, Bounty & Macquarie Is

SKYLARK
Alauda arvensis
Snares, Auckland & Campbell Is

PM/DOC

PR/DOC

DUNNOCK (HEDGE SPARROW)
Prunella modularis
Auckland, Campbell & Antipodes Is

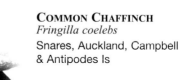

♀

MFS

♂

COMMON CHAFFINCH
Fringilla coelebs
Snares, Auckland, Campbell
& Antipodes Is

TS

♀

DV

EUROPEAN GOLDFINCH
Carduelis carduelis
Auckland, Campbell & Antipodes Is

♂

♀

HOUSE SPARROW
Passer domesticus
Auckland & Campbell Is

WINTERING BIRDS & VAGRANTS

LAYSAN ALBATROSS
Phoebetria immutabilis
S Indian Ocean

CAPE GANNET
Sula capensis
St Paul Is

LITTLE PIED CORMORANT (SHAG)
Phalacrocorax melanoleucos
Snares Is

WHITE STORK
Ciconia ciconia
Marion Is

STRIATED HERON
Butorides striata
Tristan da Cunha

WHITE-FACED HERON
Ardea novaehollandiae
Snares, Auckland & Macquarie Is

GREAT EGRET
Ardea alba
Tristan da Cunha,
Snares & Campbell Is

SNOWY EGRET
Egretta thula
Tristan da Cunha

TC

CATTLE EGRET
Bubulcus ibis
South Georgia, S Shetland, S Orkney,
Tristan da Cunha , Marion, Crozet,
Amsterdam, St Paul & Snares Is

Non-breeding plumage

Breeding plumage

CANADA GOOSE
Branta canadensis
Snares Is

WINTERING BIRDS & VAGRANTS

MANED DUCK
Chenonetta jubata
Snares Is

GRAY TEAL
Anas gracilis
Snares Is

BLUE-WINGED TEAL
Anas discors
South Georgia Is

EURASIAN COOT
Fulica atra
Macquarie Is

WEKA RAIL
Gallirallus australis
Introduced Macquarie Is by sealers as a food source, but the 1.5-lb flightless rails preyed on birds & eggs, thus they were removed in the 1990s

PURPLE SWAMPHEN (PUKEKO)
Porphyrio porphyrio
Campbell Is

PURPLE GALLINULE
Porphyrio martinica
Tristan da Cunha

AS

BLACK-BELLIED (GRAY) PLOVER
Pluvialis squatarola
Macquarie Is

AS

Breeding plumage   Winter plumage

MASKED LAPWING
Vanellus miles
Snares, Campbell & Bounty Is

RINGED PLOVER
Charadrius hiaticula
Marion Is

WINTERING BIRDS & VAGRANTS

BLACK-TAILED GODWIT
Limosa limosa
Auckland Is

WHIMBREL
Numenius phaeopus
Marion, Crozet, St Paul
& Amsterdam Is

AS

UPLAND SANDPIPER
Bartramia longicauda
Tristan da Cunha & S Shetland Is

AS

RUDDY TURNSTONE
Arenaria interpres
Tristan da Cunha, Marion, Crozet, Amsterdam, St
Paul, Kerguelen, Snares, Auckland, Campbell,
Antipodes & Macquarie Is

SPOTTED SANDPIPER
Actitis macularius
Tristan da Cunha & S Georgia

AS

RED KNOT
Calidris canutus
Amsterdam, St Paul, Auckland,
Campbell & Macquarie Is

AS

WHITE-RUMPED SANDPIPER
Calidris fuscicollis
Tristan da Cunha

AS

PECTORAL SANDPIPER
Calidris melanotos
Antarctic Peninsula, Tristan da Cunha
& Marion Is

AS

SANDERLING
Calidris alba
Amsterdam, St Paul & Kerguelen Is

AS

WHITE-HEADED STILT
Himantopus leucocephalus
Bounty & Macquarie Is

AS

Winter plumage

AS

RED (GRAY) PHALAROPE
Phalaropus fulicarius
Marion, S Orkney Is & Antarctic Peninsula

Breeding plumage

WILSON'S PHALAROPE
Phalaropus tricolor
S Orkney Is & Antarctic Peninsula

AS

WINTERING BIRDS & VAGRANTS

SOUTH ISLAND PIED OYSTERCATCHER
Haematopus finschi
Snares & Campbell Is

BLACK-BILLED GULL
Larus bulleri
Snares Is

LESSER BLACK-BACKED GULL
Larus fuscus
Marion Is

PARASITIC JAEGER (ARCTIC SKUA)
Stercorarius parasiticus
Bouvetøya, S Orkney & Marion Is

AS

Dark morph

POMARINE JAEGER
Stercorarius pomarinus
Southern Ocean &
Antarctica

COMMON CUCKOO
Cuculus canorus
Marion & Crozet Is

COMMON NIGHTHAWK
Chordeiles minor
Tristan da Cunha

AS

BROAD-BILLED ROLLER (DOLLARBIRD)
Eurystomus glaucurus
Kerguelen Is

RED-BACKED SHRIKE
Lanius collurio
Marion Is

BARN SWALLOW
Hirundo rustica
Tristan, Marion & Crozet Is

AS

WELCOME SWALLOW
Hirundo neoxena
Snares, Auckland, Campbell
& Macquarie Is

GRAY WARBLER
Gerygone igata
Snares Is

JLK

EUROPEAN GREENFINCH
Carduelis chloris
Snares Is

JLK

WINTERING BIRDS & VAGRANTS (Not illustrated)

Hoary-headed Grebe *Poliocephalus poliocephalus* Snares Is

Leach's Storm-Petrel *Hydrobates pelagicus* Tristan & S Shetland Is

Australasian Gannet *Sula serrator* Marion, Crozet, Amsterdam, St Paul, Auckland & Snares Is

Great Cormorant *Phalacrocorax carbo* Snares, Campbell & Macquarie Is

Pied Cormorant *Phalacrocorax varius* Snares Is

Intermediate Egret *Ardea intermedia* Marion Is

Black-crowned Night-Heron *Nycticorax nycticorax* Amsterdam & St Paul Is (PP 100)

Cocoi Heron *Ardea cocoi* Gough Is (PP 122)

Black-necked Swan *Cygnus melancoryphus* S Shetland Is & Antarctic Pen (PP 102)

Chiloe Wigeon *Anas flavirostris* S Shetland, S Orkney, S Georgia Is & Antarctic Peninsula (PP 107)

Eaton's Pintail *Anas eatoni* Marion Is (PP 51)

South Georgia Pintail *Anas g. georgica* S Shetland Is (PP 51)

Yellow-billed Pintail *Anas georgica spincauda* S Shetland, S Orkney & Gough Is; Antarctic Peninsula (PP 109)

Cinnamon Teal *Anas cyanoptera* S Georgia Is (PP 108)

Lake Duck *Oxyura vittata* S Shetland Is (PP 124)

Swamp Harrier *Circus approximans* Snares, Auckland, Campbell & Macquarie Is

Turkey Vulture *Cathartes aura* S Georgia Is (PP 109)

Peregrine Falcon *Falco peregrinus* Amsterdam & St Paul Is (PP 112)

Eurasian Hobby *Falco subbuteo* Amsterdam & St Paul Is

Baillon's Crake *Porzana pusilla* Macquarie Is

Paint-billed Crake *Neocrex erythrops* Tristan da Cunha

Corncrake *Crex crex* Marion Is

Bar-tailed Godwit *Limosa lapponica* St Paul, Amseterdam, Snares, Auckland, Campbell, Antipodes & Macquarie Is

Hudsonian Godwit *Limosa haemastica* Campbell Is

Rufous-chested Dotterel *Charadrius modestus* Tristan & S Georgia (PP 114)

Baird's Sandpiper *Calidris bairdi* S. Orkney Is (PP 127)

Least Sandpiper *Calidris minutilla* S. Orkney Is

Spur-winged Lapwing *Vanellus spinosus* Macquarie Is

Blacksmith Plover *Vanellus armatus* Marion Is

Latham's Snipe *Gallinago hardwickii* Snares & Macquarie Is

Three-banded Plover *Charadrius tricollaris* Marion Is

Greater Sandplover *Charadrius l. leschenaultii* Amsterdam, St Paul & Kerguelen Is

Pacific (Asian) Golden-Plover *Pluvialis fulva* Auckland Is

Common Greenshank *Tringa nebularia* Marion, Crozet, Amsterdam, St Paul, Kerguelen, Heard, Snares, Campbell & Macquarie Is

Solitary Sandpiper *Tringa solitaria* Tristan da Cunha

Wood Sandpiper *Tringa glareola* Marion Is

Terek Sandpiper *Xenus cinereus* Marion & Crozet Is
Common Sandpiper *Actitis hypoleucos* Marion, Crozet, Amsterdam, St Paul & Kerguelen Is
Gray-tailed Tattler *Heteroscelus brevipes* Amsterdam & St Paul Is
Sharp-tailed Sandpiper *Calidris acuminata* Tristan, Snares & Auckland Is
Curlew Sandpiper *Calidris ferruginea* Amsterdam, St Paul, Kerguelen & Auckland Is
Little Stint *Calidris minuta* Marion Is
Red-necked Stint *Calidris ruficollis* Auckland Is
Least Seedsnipe *Thinocorus rumicivoros* S Shetland Is (PP 114)
Yellow-legged Gull *Larus cachinnans* Crozet Is
Hartlaub's Gull *Larus hartlaubi* Marion Is (Unconfirmed)
Franklin's Gull *Larus pipixcan* Tristan da Cunha, Marion & S Georgia Is
Sabine's Gull *Larus sabini* Marion & Crozet Is
Black-fronted Tern *Sterna albostriata* Snares Is
Cape Turtle-Dove *Streptopelia capicola* Marion Is
European Turtle-Dove *Streptopelia turtur* Marion Is
Laughing Turtle-Dove *Streptopelia senegalensis* Marion Is
Oriental Cuckoo *Cuculus saturatus* Snares Is
Pallid Cuckoo *Cuculus pallidus* Macquarie Is
Lesser Cuckoo *Cuculus poliocephalus* Amsterdam & St Paul Is
Red-chested Cuckoo *Cuculus solitarius* Amsterdam & St Paul Is
Shining Bronze-Cuckoo *Cuculus saturatus* Snares, Auckland & Macquarie Is
Long-tailed Cuckoo *Eudynamys taitensis* Snares & Auckland Is
Barn Owl *Tyto alba* S Georgia Is (PP 117)
Southern Boobook *Ninox novaeseelandiae* Snares Is
White-throated Needletail *Hirundapus caudacutus* Snares, Campbell & Macquarie Is
Common Swift *Apus apus* Marion Is
Fork-tailed Swift *Apus pacificus* Campbell & Macquarie Is
Austral Negrito *Lessonia rufa* Antarctic Peninsula (PP 129)
Chilean Swallow *Tachycineta leucopyga* S Georgia Is & Antarctica (PP 118)
Bank Swallow (Sand Martin) *Riparia riparia* Marion & Crozet Is
Tree Martin *Hirundo nigricans* Marion & Snares Is
Northern House Martin *Delichon urbica* Marion Is
Long-tailed Meadowlark *Sturnella loyca* S Georgia Is (PP 118)
Yellow Wagtail *Motacilla flava* Marion Is
Common Whitethroat *Sylvia communis* Marion Is
Willow Warbler *Phylloscopus trochilus* Marion Is
Mountain Chat *Oenanthe monticola* Marion Is
Common Waxbill *Estrilda astrild* Amsterdam Is: Intentionally released— currently about 50 breeding pairs

MAMMALS

MARINE MAMMALS

Cetaceans can be especially difficult to identify because many show little of themselves and they are often encountered in heavy seas. Some, such as most of the seldom-seen beaked whales, remain mysterious to this day, and what little is known of a number of species is derived mainly from an occasional beached carcass. All southern marine mammals are illustrated except for Andrew's Beaked Whale (*Mesoplodon bowdoini*), Hector's Beaked Whale (*Mesoplodon hectori*) and Shepherd's Beaked Whale (*Tasmacetus shepherdi*), the latter of which has been seen alive on but a handful of occasions. Weights and measurements of all species are expressed as maximum.

Recent work suggests that as many as three distinct types of Killer Whales occur in Antarctic waters. Type A whales represent the familiar Killer Whale with a medium-sized white eyepatch oriented parallel to the body axis and no dorsal cape. These summer visitors seemingly prey mainly on Minke Whales and frequent offshore ice-free water. The type B whale eyepatch is also oriented parallel to the body axis, but it is at least twice as large, and the whales show a dorsal cape. These Orcas regularly occur in pack-ice, preying primarily on seals. Type C whales have a small forward-slanted eyepatch, a dorsal cape, and commonly venture into dense pack-ice, where they apparently prey mostly on Antarctic Toothfish. The white regions on the latter two Orcas often appear yellowish due to diatom growth. Based on appearance, behavior, diet, habitat preference and genetics, clearly three Killer Whale types occur in Antarctica, but whether these all represent distinct species remains to be seen.

INTRODUCED MAMMALS

Prior to human arrival, all Subantarctic islands were devoid of terrestrial mammals, though a Brazilian Free-tailed Bat (*Tadarida brasiliensis*) once reached the Falklands. Subsequent mammal introductions proved disastrous. Many were introduced as a food source, with rabbits, hares, goats, sheep, ponies, mules and cattle detrimental to the fragile ecosystems by degrading indigenous vegetation and causing erosion. Fortunately, hoofed stock has since been removed from most islands. While some islands are now rabbit free, lagomorphs persist elsewhere, resulting in a complete absence of native vegetation in areas. Feral pigs continue to be a major problem, preying even on albatross chicks. However, damage done by all introduced exotics combined pales in comparison to the havoc caused by feral cats and Norway and Black rats. Cats, rats and even House Mice have exterminated many smaller birds as breeding species from numerous islands. Considerable effort has been devoted to removing cats, with Marion and Macquarie Islands recently designated devoid of cats. Following an extremely ambitious predator eradication program by the New Zealand Department of Conservation, Campbell Island was declared free of rats in 2003.

New Zealand (Hooker's) Sea Lion
Phocarctos hookeri
Bull 990 lb (450kg): 11' (3.3m). Female 350 lb (160kg): 6'7" (2.0m)
NZ: Auckland, Campbell & Snares Is
- Bull has massive roundish head,
  w/ short, blunt muzzle
- Heavy mane of long coarse hair on
  huge neck & shoulders
- Yellowish to creamy-white female has darker
  areas on snout & upper fore flippers

Pup

South American Sea Lion
Otaria flavescens
Bull 770 lb (350kg): 9'2" (2.8m). Female 310 lb (140kg): 7'3" (2.2m)
South America & Falkland Is
- Bull has massive head & neck
- Impressive mane extends to shoulders
- Short, blunt, up-turned snout
- Males normally darker than females

TC

77

ANTARCTIC FUR SEAL
Arctocephalus gazella

Bull 415-440 lb (aver 200kg): 6'7" (2m). Female 88 lb (40kg): 4'5" (1.4m)

S Georgia, S Orkney, S Shetland, S Sandwich, Bouvetøya, Marion, Kerguelen, Heard & Macquarie Is; Antarctic Penisula

- Short, broad, blunt snout compared to other fur seals
- Bull has long dark silver-streaked mane
- Female paler, especially ventrally
- 1% of population consists of distinct golden morph

Pup

Golden morph

SUBANTARCTIC (AMSTERDAM) FUR SEAL
Arctocephalus tropicalis

Bull 350 lb (160kg): 6'7" (2.0m). Female 110 lb (50kg): 4'7" (1.4m)

Tristan da Cunha, Gough, P Edward, Marion, Crozet, Amsterdam, St Paul & Macquarie Is

- Both sexes have orange-tinged or cream-colored face & chest
- Bull has small prominent "crest"
- Relatively smaller flippers than Antarctic Fur Seal

Pup

BS

BS

BH

BH

New Zealand Fur Seal
Arctocephalus forsteri
Bull 400 lb (180kg): 8'2" (2.5m). Female 110 lb (50kg): 4'11" (1.5m)
Tasmania & NZ: Chatham, Snares, Auckland, Campbell, Antipodes, Bounty & Macquarie Is
• Long, straight, sharply pointed snout & large fleshy nose
• Rather heavy-chested bull has moderately developed mane
• Female pale grayish-olive dorsally & paler ventrally

South African (Cape) Fur Seal
Arctocephalus pusillus
Bull 790 lb (360kg): 7.5' (2.3m). Female 260 lb (120kg): 5'7" (1.7m)
Southern Africa south to Marion Is
• Largest, most robust fur
  seal— recalls a sea lion
• Bull very heavy chested,
  w/ thick, dark mane
• Much smaller female mainly
  brownish silver-gray

Pup

PR

South American Fur Seal
Arctocephalus australis
Bull 440 lb (200kg): 6'3" (1.9m). Female 110 lb (50kg): 4'7" (1.4m)
S South Amer & Falkland Is
• Robust bull has prominent mane of longer, paler hair
• Moderately long, pointed snout may appear slightly upturned

Southern Elephant Seal
Mirounga leonina

Bull 11,000 lb (5000kg): 16'6" (5m). Female 2000 lb (900kg): 10' (3m)

S Amer & Falkland, S Shetland, S Orkney, S Sandwich, Bouvetøya & most Subantarctic Is; a few pup in Antarctica

- Largest seal
- Massive bull has prominent proboscis & heavily scarred neck
- Round-faced female has very large eyes

♀   Pup

♂

♀   ♂

♀

Weddell Seal
Leptonychotes weddellii

Larger female to 1200 lb (550kg): 11' (3.3m)

S Shetland Is & Antarctica- most southerly breeding mammal

- Proportionally small head & flippers
- Coat pattern varies considerably
- Whiskers often distinctly curled
- Favors fast-ice over pack-ice

CRABEATER SEAL
Lobodon carcinophaga
Slightly larger female 510 lb (230kg): 8'8" (2.7m)
Antarctic pack-ice
- Distinct up-turned snout
- Often scarred due to leopard seal attacks
- Color variable from blackish to silvery-white
- Often more than one seal on ice-floe

ROSS SEAL
Ommatophoca rossii
Slightly larger female 440 lb (200kg): 7'10" (2.4m)
Antarctic pack-ice
- Smallest Antarctic seal
- Large, protruding eyes & tiny teeth
- Dark streaks extend from chin to chest
- Often points head up w/ open mouth & neck greatly inflated
- Favors dense pack-ice

LEOPARD SEAL
Hydruga leptonyx

Larger female 1300 lb (590kg): 12' (3.6m)

Antarctic pack-ice

- Massive head, w/ huge gape
- Spotted coat
- 'Sinister, reptilian' appearance
- Large pectoral flippers
- Very inquisitive, but can be dangerous

COMMERSON'S DOLPHIN
Cephalorhynchus commersonii
190 lb (86kg): 5'9" (1.74m)
S South Amer: Falkland & Kerguelen Is
- Black head, flippers & flukes
- Rounded black fin
- Larger Kerguelen dolphin less boldly marked
- Inshore species
- Readily approaches boats & leaps often

Calf

SW

Calf

DH

Kerguelen Is

HOURGLASS DOLPHIN
Lagenorhynchus cruciger
Wt unknown, but probably 200-250 lb (90-113kg): 6'2" (1.9m)
- Black & white, w/ distinct white hourglass pattern
- Only dolphin in Antarctic waters w/ fin
- Highly pelagic, occurring well away from shore
- Commonly leaps & bow rides

RP

PE

DUSKY DOLPHIN
Lagenorhynchus obscurus
187 lbs (85kg): 6'11" (2.1m)
- Falcate bicolored fin black in front & pale gray in back
- White throat & 2 whitish flank stripes
- Acrobatic, w/ high somersaults & commonly bow rides

DH

DB

FN

BT

PEALE'S DOLPHIN
Lagenorhynchus australis
Wt unknown, but probably about 250 lb (113kg): 7'1" (2.1m)
S South Amer & Falkland Is
- Dark face, w/ chin black to behind eye
- White 'armpit' patch behind flipper
- Single diagonal white flank patch
- Coastal inshore waters, often in kelp
- Acrobatic & may bow ride

TP

TC

TP

TC

BOTTLENOSE DOLPHIN
Tursiops truncatus

Up to 1,100 lb (500kg): 12'6" (3.8m)

- Robust, w/ short to medium-length beak
- Subdued gray coloration
- Mainly warm water species, but has stranded twice in the Falkland Is

SW

SPECTACLED PORPOISE
Phocoena dioptrica

Wt unknown, but probably 250 lb (115kg): 7'5" (2.3m)

- Black dorsally & white ventrally, w/ belly often visible
- Black eye patch outlined by white 'spectacles'
- Male fin may have broadly rounded tip; smaller female fin low & triangular
- Dorsal flipper & fluke either black or white, but not sex related
- Black lips

Calf

JB & FST

PO

Calf

PO

Calf

85

SOUTHERN RIGHT WHALE DOLPHIN
Lissodelphis peronii
260 lb (116kg): 9'9" (3m)
- Very slender, w/ no fin
- Black above & white ventrally,
  w/ white forehead & flippers
- Often swims very fast in groups
  of 100-200, even 1000+

IV

BT

RP

LONG-FINNED PILOT WHALE
Globicephala melas
2.5 tons: 21' (6.3m)
- Rounded, bulbous forehead
- Broad-based fin positioned well forward on body
- Exceptionally long, tapered flippers about 1/4th body length
- Light streak behind eye & pale saddle behind fin

FN

FN

BH

PE

SOUTHERN BOTTLENOSE WHALE
Hyperoodon planifrons
Wt unknown, but probably 6-8 tons: 25' (7.5m)
- Bulbous forehead & distinct beak
- Long robust body tan to bluish-black
- Melon may be pale
- Prominent falcate fin
- No notch in flukes

RP

AB

ARNOUX'S BEAKED WHALE
Beradius arnuxii
Wt unknown, but probably 7-10 tons: 32' (9.8m)
- Large bulbous melon
- Dark colored, but may appear brown or even orange
- Lower mandible longer than upper, w/ front teeth visible at tip
- Many linear scars
- Small fin set far back on body
- Beaked whale most often encountered in the ice

JK

GRAY'S BEAKED WHALE
Mesoplodon grayi
1.2 tons: 19' (5.7m)

PE

- Long white beak; forehead often lifted clear of water
- Long, slender body & small head
- Small falcate fin
- May porpoise or breach

PE

87

STRAP-TOOTHED WHALE
Mesoplodon layardii

Wt probably 1.1-1.5 tons: 20' (6.2m)

- Long, slender beak mostly white
- Dark face mask
- Small fin
- Female lacks teeth
- Two male teeth to 12" (30.5cm) long curl around upper jaw, preventing mouth from being fully opened

PO

RP

RP

♂

CUVIER'S BEAKED WHALE
Ziphius cavirostris

3.3 tons: 23' (7m)

- Robust body & small head white in adult male
- Color variable; blue-gray, purplish-black, pale brown to white
- Relatively small, falcate fin set about 2/3rds back on body
- 2 teeth at tip of male lower jaw point somewhat forward & upward
- May have long & circular scars

TP

TP

KILLER WHALE (ORCA)
Orcinus orca

6 tons: 30' (9m)

- White eye patch, saddle & belly
- White areas may appear yellowish due to algae (diatom) growth
- Bull triangular fin to 6' tall
- Large, paddle-shaped flippers
- Inquisitive & commonly spyhops

SPERM WHALE
Physeter macrocephalus

Bull 60 tons: 60' (18.3m). Female 27.5 tons; >36' (11m)

- S-shaped blowhole on left side of head; bushy blow forward & to left
- Square head 1/3 body length
- Hump-like dorsal, w/ knuckle-like ridges along tail stalk
- Wrinkled, prune-like skin
- Triangular flukes lifted high when diving deep
- Large bulls most likely to occur in higher latitudes

FN

FN

FN

FN

FN

Pygmy Right Whale
Caperea marginata
Wt unknown, but probably 3.0-3.5 tons: 21' (6.4m)
- Smallest, least known baleen whale
- Strongly arched jaw line
- Lacks head callosities
- Dark-colored narrow flippers, w/ rounded tips
- Prominent falcate dorsal fin

RP

RP

RP

Dwarf Minke Whale
Balaenoptera acutorostrata
Wt unknown, but probably about 7 tons: 26' (7.8m)
- Much smaller & paler overall than Antarctic Minke
- Sharply pointed head & falcate fin
- Extensive white on flippers
- Less likely to be encountered in pack-ice than Antarctic Minke

FN

FN

FN

91

ANTARCTIC MINKE WHALE
Balaenoptera bonaerensis
10 tons: 35' (10.7m)
- Extremely pointed snout
- Prominent falcate fin
- Does not raise flukes when diving
- Low bushy blow
- Spyhops in pack-ice

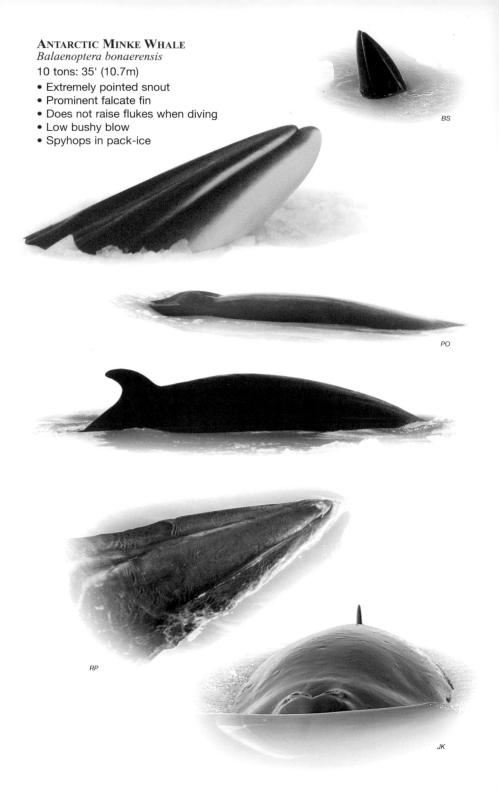

BS

PO

RP

JK

92

SEI WHALE
Balaenoptera borealis
50 tons: 64' (19.5m)

- Tall, sickle-shaped fin
- Single ridge extends from splash guard to rostrum tip
- Blow & large falcate fin may appear on surface nearly simultaneously
- May have roundish white or gray scars caused by cookie-cutter sharks

FIN WHALE
Balaenoptera physalus
130 tons: 89' (27.1m)

- 2nd largest whale, w/ prominent fin
- Fin appears just after narrow 15-20' blow
- Left jaw black & right lower jaw white
- Pale chevron pattern behind head often visible from above
- Rarely shows flukes

BLUE WHALE
Balaenoptera musculus
200 tons: 110' (33.3m)

- Broad, flattened U-shaped head
- Mottled pale gray-blue
- Prominent splash guard in front of huge blowholes
- Tiny fin set well back on body
- 20-40' tall columnar spout
- Often throws flukes when diving

HUMPBACK WHALE
Megaptera novaeangliae
45 tons: 52-56' (16-17m)

- Huge black or white flippers 1/3 body length
- Knobby protuberances on head
- Arches (humps) back before lifting flukes & diving
- Flukes serrated along trailing edge
- Unique fluke pattern facilitates individual identification
- Inquisitive & active on surface
- May breach repeatedly

FN*

Calf

FN

BH

JJ

SOUTHERN RIGHT WHALE
Eubalaena australis

Larger female 100 tons: 56' (17m)

- V-shaped blow
- Broad back lacking dorsal fin
- Strongly arched jaw line visible on surface
- Yellow-brown head callosities unique to each individual
- Slow swimming, but surprising acrobatic, even breaching

INTRODUCED MAMMALS

EUROPEAN RABBIT
Oryctolagus cuniculus
Falklands & many
Subantarctic Is

TC

NORWAY RAT
Rattus norvegicus
Falklands & many
Subantarctic Is

PM

PATAGONIAN GRAY FOX
Dusicyon griseys
Introduced in the early
1930s from South America
to 5 West Falkland islands

FERAL CAT
Felis catus
Falklands & many Subantarctic Is

MARINE OTTER
Lutra felina
Introduced into the Falkland Is in the
1930s from southern Chile; current
status unknown

INTRODUCED MAMMALS

AUCKLAND PIG
Sus scrofa
Auckland Is

GUANACO
Lama guanicoe
Introduced 1862 & 1871
into the Falkland Is, &
again in 1937. In the
1980s, some 140
inhabited Staats Island

REINDEER
Rangifer tarandus
Norwegian stock introduced S Georgia
between 1911 & 1925. Current
population about 2000, w/ periodic
culling required. In 1955, reindeer
released Kerguelen Is (Grande Terre)

MOUFLON
Ovis musimon
Wild sheep from
Corsica presently
restricted to Ill Haute,
Kerguelen Is

BREEDING BIRDS OF THE FALKLAND ISLANDS

WHITE-TUFTED (ROLLAND'S) GREBE 100

SILVERY GREBE 100

BLACK-CROWNED NIGHT-HERON 100

KING PENGUIN 5

NORTHERN GENTOO PENGUIN 7

ROCKHOPPER PENGUIN 8

MACARONI PENGUIN 10

MAGELLANIC PENGUIN 13

BLACK-BROWED ALBATROSS 23

SOUTHERN GIANT-PETREL 29

NORTHERN GIANT-PETREL* 30

WHITE-CHINNED PETREL 36

GREATER SHEARWATER 37

SOOTY SHEARWATER 38

SLENDER-BILLED PRION 40

FAIRY PRION* 41

WILSON'S STORM-PETREL 42

GRAY-BACKED STORM-PETREL 43

BLACK-BELLIED STORM-PETREL* 44

COMMON DIVING-PETREL 45

IMPERIAL (KING) SHAG 101

ROCK SHAG 101

COSCOROBA SWAN 102

BLACK-NECKED SWAN 102

GREATER UPLAND GOOSE 103

FERAL DOMESTIC GOOSE 103

GREATER KELP GOOSE 104

RUDDY-HEADED GOOSE 105

ASHY-HEADED GOOSE 105

FALKLAND FLIGHTLESS STEAMERDUCK ..106

FLYING STEAMERDUCK 106

PATAGONIAN CRESTED DUCK 107

CHILOE WIGEON 107

MALLARD 64

CINNAMON TEAL 108

RED SHOVELER* 108

SILVER (VERSICOLOR) TEAL 108

SPECTACLED (YELLOW-BILLED) TEAL 109

YELLOW-BILLED PINTAIL 109

TURKEY VULTURE 109

RED-BACKED HAWK (BUZZARD) 110

STRIATED CARACARA (JOHNNY ROOK) ...111

CRESTED CARACARA 111

PEREGRINE FALCON 112

AMERICAN KESTREL* 112

MAGELLANIC OYSTERCATCHER 113

BLACKISH OYSTERCATCHER 113

MAGELLANIC SNIPE 113

CORDILLERAN (FUEGAN) SNIPE+

TWO-BANDED PLOVER 114

RUFOUS-CHESTED DOTTEREL 114

LEAST SEEDSNIPE* 114

KELP GULL 56

DOLPHIN GULL 115

BROWN-HOODED GULL 115

SOUTH AMERICAN TERN 116

FALKLAND (BROWN) SKUA 116

BARN OWL 117

SHORT-EARED OWL 117

TUSSOCKBIRD (BLACKISH CINCLODES) ...117

FALKLAND (CORRENDERA) PIPIT 117

DARK-FACED GROUND-TYRANT 118

FALKLAND (AUSTRAL) THRUSH 118

CHILEAN SWALLOW 118

LONG-TAILED MEADOWLARK 118

COBB'S WREN 119

FALKLAND GRASS WREN 119

HOUSE SPARROW 65

BLACK-CHINNED SISKIN 119

BLACK-THROATED FINCH 119

*Possible breeder

+Possible breeder *Gallinago stricklandii* (Not pictured)

FALKLAND ISLANDS BREEDING BIRDS

WHITE-TUFTED (ROLLAND'S) GREBE
Rollandia r. rolland

TC

SILVERY GREBE
Podiceps o. occipitalis

TC

BLACK-CROWNED NIGHT-HERON
Nycticorax nycticorax falklandicus

Juvenile

FALKLAND ISLANDS BREEDING BIRDS

IMPERIAL (KING) SHAG
Phalacrocorax atriceps albiventer
- Similar to Antarctic Shag, but demarcation
  between black & white of face extends across gape
- Lacks white upper back
- Ragged white shoulders

Juvenile

ROCK SHAG
Phalacrocorax magellanicus

Juvenile

TC

101

FALKLAND ISLANDS BREEDING BIRDS

COSCOROBA SWAN
Coscoroba coscoroba

BLACK-NECKED SWAN
Cygnus melancoryphus

Juvenile

♂

♀

FALKLAND ISLANDS BREEDING BIRDS

GREATER UPLAND GOOSE
Chloephaga picta leucoptera

FERAL DOMESTIC GOOSE
Anser anser

GREATER KELP GOOSE
Chloephaga hybrida malvinarum

♂

♀

♂

♀

♂

♂

Juvenile

FALKLAND ISLANDS BREEDING BIRDS

RUDDY-HEADED GOOSE
Chloephaga rubidiceps

- Sexes alike, w/ orange legs & feet
- Similar to larger female Upland Goose, but more finely barred ventrally

♀   ♂

ASHY-HEADED GOOSE
Chloephaga poliocephala

FALKLAND ISLANDS BREEDING BIRDS

FALKLAND FLIGHTLESS STEAMERDUCK
Tachyeres brachypterus

FLYING STEAMERDUCK
Tachyeres patachonicus

FALKLAND ISLANDS BREEDING BIRDS

PATAGONIAN CRESTED DUCK
Anas (Lophonetta) s. specularioides

CHILOE WIGEON
Anas sibilatrix

FALKLAND ISLANDS BREEDING BIRDS

CINNAMON TEAL
Anas c. cyanoptera

♂

♀

♂

♂

SILVER (VERSICOLOR) TEAL
Anas versicolor fretensis

RED SHOVELER
Anas platalea
Possible breeder

♂

♀

FALKLAND ISLANDS BREEDING BIRDS

Speckled (Yellow-billed) Teal
Anas flavirostris

Yellow-billed Pintail
Anas georgica spinicauda

Turkey Vulture
Cathartes aura falklandicus

Juvenile

FALKLAND ISLANDS BREEDING BIRDS

RED-BACKED HAWK (BUZZARD)
Buteo p. polyosoma

♂

TC

TC

♀

Dark morph

♀

TC

Immature

TC

♀

Juvenile

♂

TC

Pale morph

110

FALKLAND ISLANDS BREEDING BIRDS

STRIATED CARACARA (JOHNNY ROOK)
Phalcoboenus australis

Juvenile

Juvenile

CRESTED CARACARA
Caracara p. plancus

FALKLAND ISLANDS BREEDING BIRDS

PEREGRINE FALCON
Falco peregrinus cassini

TC

AMERICAN KESTREL
Falco sparverius
Possible breeder

AS

FALKLAND ISLANDS BREEDING BIRDS

MAGELLANIC OYSTERCATCHER
Haematopus leucopodus

BLACKISH OYSTERCATCHER
Haematopus ater

MAGELLANIC SNIPE
Gallinago paraguaiae magellanica

113

FALKLAND ISLANDS BREEDING BIRDS

TWO-BANDED PLOVER
Charadrius falklandicus

Juvenile

TC

BH

RUFOUS-CHESTED DOTTEREL
Charadrius modestus

TC

♂

♀

LEAST SEEDSNIPE
Thinocorus rumicivorus
Possible breeder

FALKLAND ISLANDS BREEDING BIRDS

DOLPHIN GULL
Larus scoresbii

Juvenile

Non-breeding plumage

BROWN-HOODED GULL
Larus maculipennis

Immature

TC

FALKLAND ISLANDS BREEDING BIRDS

SOUTH AMERICAN TERN
Sterna hirundinacea

TC

Non-breeding plumage

TC

FALKLAND (BROWN) SKUA
Stercorarius (Catharacta) a. antarcticus

FALKLAND ISLANDS BREEDING BIRDS

BARN OWL
Tyto alba tuidara

SHORT-EARED OWL
Asio flammeus sanfordi

TUSSOCKBIRD (BLACKISH CINCLODES)
Cinclodes a. antarcticus

FALKLAND (CORRENDERA) PIPIT
Anthus correndera grayi

FALKLAND ISLANDS BREEDING BIRDS

DARK-FACED GROUND-TYRANT
Muscisaxicola m. maclovianus

TC

FALKLAND (AUSTRAL) THRUSH
Turdus f. falcklandii

Juvenile

TC

CHILEAN SWALLOW
Tachycineta meyeni

LONG-TAILED MEADOWLARK
Sturnella loyca falklandica

♀

♂

TC

118

FALKLAND ISLANDS BREEDING BIRDS

FALKLAND GRASS WREN
Cistothorus platensis falklandicus

COBB'S WREN
Troglodytes cobbi

TC

TC

BLACK-CHINNED SISKIN
Carduelis barbata

TC

BLACK-THROATED FINCH
Melanodera m. melanodera

♂

♀

TC

119

WINTERING SPECIES & VAGRANTS

GREAT GREBE 122

PIED-BILLED GREBE 122

EMPEROR PENGUIN 4

ADÉLIE PENGUIN 6

CHINSTRAP PENGUIN 7

ROYAL PENGUIN 10

SNARES PENGUIN 11

ERECT-CRESTED PENGUIN 11

WANDERING ALBATROSS 16

SOUTHERN ROYAL ALBATROSS 19

WHITE-CAPPED ALBATROSS 21

GRAY-HEADED ALBATROSS 24

BULLER'S ALBATROSS 25

YELLOW-NOSED ALBATROSS 25

LIGHT-MANTLED SOOTY ALBATROSS . . .27

SOOTY ALBATROSS 28

ANTARCTIC FULMAR 30

ANTARCTIC PETREL 30

CAPE PETREL (CAPE PIGEON) 31

SNOW PETREL 31

WHITE-HEADED PETREL 32

ATLANTIC PETREL 33

MOTTLED PETREL 33

KERGUELEN PETREL 35

SOFT-PLUMAGED PETREL 34

GREAT-WINGED PETREL 34

GRAY PETREL 35

LITTLE SHEARWATER 37

ANTARCTIC PRION 39

BROAD-BILLED PRION 40

BLUE PETREL 42

WHITE-FACED STORM-PETREL 43

BLACK-BELLIED STORM-PETREL 44

WHITE-BELLIED STORM-PETREL 44

SOUTH GEORGIAN DIVING-PETREL . . .45

RED-LEGGED CORMORANT 122

COCOI HERON 122

STRAITED HERON 66

GREAT EGRET 67

SNOWY EGRET 67

CATTLE EGRET 67

MAGUARI STORK 122

BLACK-FACED IBIS 123

ROSEATE SPOONBILL 123

CHILEAN FLAMINGO 123

SPECTACLED (BRONZE-WINGED) DUCK 123

WHITE-CHEEKED PINTAIL 124

ROSY-BILLED POCHARD 123

LAKE (ARGENTINE RUDDY) DUCK . . .124

BLACK-HEADED DUCK 124

CINEREOUS HARRIER 125

SHARP-SHINNED HAWK 124

CHIMANGO CARACARA 125

APLOMADO FALCON 125

PLUMBEOUS RAIL 126

AUSTRAL RAIL 126

PURPLE GALLINULE 69

RED-FRONTED COOT 125

WHITE-WINGED COOT 125

SNOWY SHEATHBILL 54

BLACK-NECKED STILT 127

AMERICAN GOLDEN-PLOVER 126

TAWNY-THROATED DOTTEREL 126

MAGELLANIC PLOVER 127

SOUTHERN LAPWING 126

WHIMBREL 70

GREATER YELLOWLEGS 127

RUDDY TURNSTONE 70

RED KNOT 70

PECTORAL SANDPIPER 70

UPLAND SANDPIPER 70	ARCTIC TERN .57
SANDERLING .71	EARED DOVE .130
WHITE-RUMPED SANDPIPER 71	BURROWING PARROT 129
BAIRD'S SANDPIPER 127	AUSTRAL PARAKEET 129
SURFBIRD 127	MAGELLANIC HORNED OWL 129
RED (GRAY) PHALAROPE 71	BURROWING OWL 129
WILSON'S PHALAROPE 71	BAR-WINGED CINCLODES 130
SOUTH POLAR SKUA 58	THORN-TAILED RAYADITO 130
CHILEAN SKUA 128	FIRE-EYED DIUCON 130
PARASITIC JAEGER 72	CATTLE TYRANT 130
LONG-TAILED JAEGER 129	AUSTRAL NEGRITO 131
BAND-TAILED GULL 128	GREAT KISKADEE 131
GRAY GULL .128	EASTERN KINGBIRD 131
ELEGANT TERN 128	CLIFF SWALLOW 131
SANDWICH TERN 128	BARN SWALLOW 73
COMMON TERN 128	RUFOUS-COLLARED SPARROW 131
ANTARCTIC TERN 57	

FALKLAND ISLANDS MARINE MAMMALS

SOUTH AMERICAN SEA LION* 77	GRAY'S BEAKED WHALE 87
SOUTH AMERICAN FUR SEAL* 79	CUVIER'S BEAKED WHALE 88
SOUTHERN ELEPHANT SEAL* 80	SOUTHERN BOTTLENOSE WHALE 87
WEDDELL SEAL 80	LONG-FINNED PILOT WHALE 86
LEOPARD SEAL 82	KILLER WHALE (ORCA) 89
COMMERSON'S DOLPHIN* 83	SPERM WHALE 90
HOURGLASS DOLPHIN 83	DWARF MINKE WHALE 91
DUSKY DOLPHIN* 84	SEI WHALE 93
PEALE'S DOLPHIN* 84	FIN WHALE 93
BOTTLENOSE DOLPHIN 85	BLUE WHALE 94
SPECTACLED PORPOISE 85	HUMPBACK WHALE 95
SOUTHERN RIGHT WHALE DOLPHIN .86	SOUTHERN RIGHT WHALE 96
ARNOUX'S BEAKED WHALE 87	PYGMY RIGHT WHALE 91
STRAP-TOOTHED WHALE 88	

*Falkland Islands breeding species

WINTERING BIRDS & VAGRANTS

GREAT GREBE
Podiceps major

TC

PIED-BILLED GREBE
Podilymbus podiceps

RED-LEGGED CORMORANT
Phalacrocorax gaimardi

COCOI (WHITE-NECKED) HERON
Ardea cocoi

MAGUARI STORK
Ciconia maguari

WINTERING BIRDS & VAGRANTS

Black-faced Ibis
Theristicus melanopis

ROSEATE SPOONBILL
Platalea ajaja

Roseate Spoonbill
Platalea ajaja

Chilean Flamingo
Phoenicopterus chilensis

Spectacled (Bronze-winged) Duck
Anas specularis

Rosy-billed Pochard
Netta peposaca

WHITE-CHEEKED PINTAIL
Anas bahamensis

LAKE (ARGENTINE RUDDY) DUCK
Oxyura vittata

♀

♂

BLACK-HEADED DUCK
Heteronetta atricapilla

♀

♂

SHARP-SHINNED HAWK
Accipiter striatus

AS

WINTERING BIRDS & VAGRANTS

APLOMADO FALCON
Falco femoralis

CINEREOUS HARRIER
Circus cinereus

CHIMANGO CARACARA
Milvago chimango

RED-FRONTED COOT
Fulica rufirons

WHITE-WINGED COOT
Fulica leucoptera

WINTERING BIRDS & VAGRANTS

AUSTRAL RAIL
Rallus antarcticus

TC

PLUMBEOUS RAIL
Pardirallus sanguinolentus

TAWNY-THROATED DOTTEREL
Eudromias ruficollis

TC

SOUTHERN LAPWING
Vanellus chilensis

Breeding plumage

AMERICAN GOLDEN-PLOVER
Pluvialis dominica

AS

Non-breeding plumage

WINTERING BIRDS & VAGRANTS

GREATER YELLOWLEGS
Tringa melanoleuca

AS

SURFBIRD
Aphriza virgata

BAIRD'S SANDPIPER
Calidris bairdi

AS

BLACK-NECKED STILT
Himantopus himantopus mexicanus

AS

MAGELLANIC PLOVER
Pluvianellus socialis

JJ

WINTERING BIRDS & VAGRANTS

BAND-TAILED (BELCHER'S) GULL
Larus belcheri

GRAY GULL
Larus modestus

ELEGANT TERN
Sterna elegans

SANDWICH TERN
Sterna sandvicensis

AS

COMMON TERN
Sterna hirundo

AS

CHILEAN SKUA
Stercorarius chilensis

BH

WINTERING BIRDS & VAGRANTS

LONG-TAILED JAEGER
Stercorarius longicaudus

AUSTRAL PARAKEET
Enicognathus ferrugineus

BURROWING PARROT
Cyanoliseus patagonus

MAGELLANIC HORNED OWL
Bubo magellanicus

BURROWING OWL
Athene cunicularia

AS

WINTERING BIRDS & VAGRANTS

EARED DOVE
Zenaida auriculata

TC

THORN-TAILED RAYADITO
Aphrastura spinicauda

BAR-WINGED CINCLODES
Cinclodes fuscus

CATTLE TYRANT
Machetornis rixosa

AS

FIRE-EYED DIUCON
Pyrope pyrope

WINTERING BIRDS & VAGRANTS

AUSTRAL (RUFOUS-BACKED) NEGRITO
Lessonia rufa

GREAT KISKADEE
Pitangus sulphuratus

EASTERN KINGBIRD
Tyrannus tyrannus

AS

CLIFF SWALLOW
Petrochelidon pyrrhonota

AS

RUFOUS-COLLARED SPARROW
Zonotrichia capensis

TC

WINTERING SPECIES & VAGRANTS (Not illustrated)

Herald Petrel *Pterodroma arminjoniana*

Cory's Shearwater *Calonectris diomedea*

Manx Shearwater *Puffinus puffinus*

European Storm-Petrel *Hydrobates pelagicus*

Magellanic Diving-Petrel *Pelecanoides magellani*

Long-winged Harrier *Circus buffoni*

Speckled Rail *Coturnicops notatus*

Red-gartered Coot *Fulica armillata*

Hudsonian Godwit *Limosa haemastica*

Eskimo Curlew *Numenius borealis*

Lesser Yellowlegs *Tringa flavipes*

Semipalmated Sandpiper *Calidris pusilla*

Stilt Sandpiper *Micropalama himantopus*

White-bellied Seedsnipe *Attagis malouinus*

Gray-headed Gull *Larus cirrocephalus*

Franklin's Gull *Larus pipixcan*

Trudeau's Tern *Sterna trudeaui*

Chilean Pigeon *Patagioenas araucana*

Ruddy Ground-Dove *Columbina talpacoti*

Dark-billed Cuckoo *Coccyzus melacoryphus*

Rufous-legged Owl *Strix rufipes*

White-collared Swift *Streptoprocne zonaris*

Ashy-tailed Swift *Chaetura andrei*

Green-backed Firecrown *S. sephaniodes*

Austral Canastero *Thripophaga anthoides*

Magellanic Tapaculo *Scytalopus magellanicus*

Rufous-tailed Plantcutter *Phytotoma rara*

White-crested Elaenia *Elaenia albiceps*

Tufted Tit-Tyrant *Anairetes parulus*

Black-billed Shrike-Tyrant *Agriornis montana*

White-browed Ground-Tyrant *M. albilora*

Fork-tailed Flycatcher *Tyrannus savana*

Patagonian Mockingbird *Mimus patagonicus*

Brown-chested Martin *Phaeoprogne tapera*

Southern Martin *Progne modesta*

Purple Martin *Progne subis*

Sand Martin *Riparia riparia*

White-rumped Swallow *Tachycineta leucorrhoa*

Blue-and-white Swallow *Tachycineta cyanoleuca*

Southern Rough-winged Swallow *S. ruficollis*

Tawny-headed Swallow *Stelgidopteryx fucata*

Wood Thrush *Hylocichla mustelina*

Mourning Sierra-Finch *Phrygilus fruticeti*

Gray-hooded Sierra-Finch *Phrygilus gayi*

Patagonian Sierra-Finch *Phrygilus patagonicus*

Yellow-bridled Finch *Melanodera xanthogramma*

SPANISH NAMES

PENGUINS

Adélie Penguin	Pingüino de Adelia
Gentoo Penguin	Pingüino papúa
Chinstrap Penguin	Pingüino barbijo-antártico
Emperor Penguin	Pingüino emperador
King Penguin	Pingüino rey
Rockhopper Penguin	Pingüino de penacho amarillo
Macaroni Penguin	Pingüino macaroni
Royal Penguin	Pingüino de Schlegel
Snares Penguin	Pingüino de las Snares
Erect-crested Penguin	Pingüino de Sclater
Fjordland Penguin	Pingüino de Fjordland
Yellow-eyed Penguin	Pingüino Ojigualdo
Magellanic Penguin	Pingüino magallánico
Humboldt Penguin	Pingüino de Humboldt
African Penguin	Pingüino del Cabo
Galapagos Penguin	Pingüino de las Galápagos
Little Penguin	Pingüino enano

ALBATROSSES

Wandering Albatross	Albatros errante
Royal Albatross	Albatros real
Black-browed Albatross	Albatros de ceja negra
Shy Albatross	Albatros de frente blanca
Gray-headed Albatross	Albatros de cabeza gris
Buller's Albatross	Albatros de Buller
Yellow-nosed Albatross	Albatros Clororrinco
Lt-mantle Sooty Albatross	Albatros oscuro de manto claro
Sooty Albatross	Albatros oscuro

PETRELS

Southern Giant-Petrel	Petrel gigante antártico
Northern Giant-Petrel	Petrel gigante subantártico
Southern Fulmar	Petrel plateado
Antarctic Petrel	Petrel antártico
Cape Petrel	Petrel moteado
Snow Petrel	Petrel de las nieves
White-headed Petrel	Fardela de frente blanca
White-chinned Petrel	Fardela negra
Great-winged Petrel	Fardela de alas grandes
Kerguelen Petrel	Petrel de las Kerguelen
Atlantic Petrel	Petrel de Schlegel
Soft-plumaged Petrel	Petrel suave
Westland Petrel	Fardela negra grande
Gray Petrel	Fardela gris
Greater Shearwater	Fardela capirotada
Flesh-footed Shearwater	Fardela negra de patas pálidas
Sooty Shearwater	Fardela negra
Short-tailed Shearwater	Fardela de Tasmania
Little Shearwater	Fardela chica
Broad-billed Prion	Fardela paloma piquiancho
Salvin's Prion	Fardela paloma de Salvin
Antarctic Prion	Fardela paloma antártico
Slender-billed Prion	Fardela paloma de pico delgado
Fairy Prion	Fardela paloma piquicorto
Fulmar Prion	Fardela paloma picogrueso
Blue Petrel	Petrel azulado

STORM-PETRELS

Wilson's Storm-Petrel	Golondrina de mar
Gray-back Storm-Petrel	G. de mar subantártica
Wt-faced Storm-Petrel	Golondrina de mar pechiblanco
Bk-bellied Storm-Petrel	G. de mar de vientre negro
Wt-bellied Storm-Petrel	G. de mar de vientre blanco

DIVING-PETRELS

S. Georgian Diving-Petrel	Patoyunco de Georgia del Sur
Common Diving-Petrel	Patoyunco de los canales

CORMORANTS

Antarctic Shag	Cormorán antártico
South Georgian Shag	Cormorán de Georgia del Sur
Macquarie Shag	Cormorán de la Macquarie
Kerguelen Shag	Cormorán de las Kerguelen
Crozet Shag	Cormorán de las Crozet
Heard Shag	Cormorán de la Heard
Campbell Shag	Cormorán de las Campbell
Auckland Shag	Cormorán de las Auckland
Bounty Shag	Cormorán de las Bounty

WATERFOWL

Australian Shelduck	Tarro australiano
Mallard	Anade azulón
Pacific Black Duck	Anade cejudo
Auckland Flightless Teal	Cerceta maorí
Campbell Flightless Teal	Cerceta maorí de Campbell
Eaton's Pintail	Anade rabudo de Eaton
South Georgian Pintail	Pato jergón grande
Speckled Teal	Pato jergón chico
Auckland Merganser	Serreta de las Auckland

FALCONS

New Zealand Falcon	Halcón de Nueva Zelandia

RAILS

Gough Moorhen	Gallineta de Gough
Auckland Rail	Rascón de Auckland
Inaccessible F. Rail	Rascóncillo de las Tristan

SHEATHBILLS

Snowy Sheathbill	Paloma antártica
Black-faced Sheathbill	Picovaina chico

SHOREBIRDS

Double-banded Dotterel	Chorlitejo bicinchado
New Zealand Snipe	Chocha de Auckland

GULLS, TERNS & SKUAS

Kelp Gull	Gaviota dominicana
Red-billed Gull	Gaviota plateada neozelandesa
Common Noddy	Gaviotín de San Félix
Antarctic Tern	Gaviotín antártico
Arctic Tern	Gaviotín ártico
Kerguelen Tern	Gaviotín de Kerguelen
White-fronted Tern	Gaviotín maorí
Sooty Tern	Gaviotín apizzarado
South Polar Skua	Salteador antártico
Brown Skua	Salteador pardo

PARAKEETS

Antipodes Parakeet	P. verde de las Antípodas
Rec-crowned Parakeet	Periquito de frontal rojo
Yellow-crown Parakeet	Periquito de frontal amarillo

PASSERINES

South Georgia Pipit	Bailarín de Georgia del Sur
New Zealand Pipit	Bailarín de Nueva Zelandia
New Zealand Bellbird	Pájaro campana de N Zelandia
Tui	Tui
Tristan Thrush	Zorzal de Tristán da Cunha
European Blackbird	Tordo europeo
Song Thrush	Tordo cantor
Auckland Tomtit	Petirrojo de isla Auckland
Snares Tomtit	Petirrojo de isla Snares
Snares Fernbird	Ave de los helechos de Snares
New Zealand Fantail	Cola de abanico de N Zelandia
Silvereye	Ojiblanco de lomo gris
Skylark	Alondra común
Common Starling	Estornino pinto
Dunnock	Acentor común
Common Chaffinch	Pinzón vulgar
European Goldfinch	Jilguero
Common Redpoll	Pardillo sizerín
Yellowhammer	Escribano cerillo
House Sparrow	Gorrión
Gough Bunting	Semillero de Gough
Tristan Bunting	Semillero ruiseñor
Grosbeak Bunting	Semillero de Wilkins

MAMMALS

New Zealand Sea Lion	Lobo marino de N Zelandia
S. American Sea Lion	Lobo marino común
Antarctic Fur Seal	Lobo fino antártico
Subantarctic Fur seal	Lobo fino subantártico
New Zealand Fur Seal	Lobo fino de Nueva Zelandia
South American Fur Seal	Lobo fino de dos pelos
South African Fur Seal	Lobo fino de Sudáfrica
Southern Elephant Seal	Elefante marino
Weddell Seal	Foca de Weddell
Crabeater Seal	Foca cangrejera
Ross Seal	Foca de Ross
Leopard Seal	Leopardo marino
Commerson's Dolphin	Tunina overa
Hourglass Dolphin	Delfín cruzado
Dusky Dolphin	Delfín oscuro
Peale's Dolphin	Delfín austral
Bottlenose Dolphin	Delfín nariz de botella
Spectacled Porpoise	Marsopa anteojillo
Arnoux's Beaked Whale	Ballena picuda de Arnoux
Strap-toothed Whale	Ballena de diente plano
Gray's Beaked Whale	Ballena picuda de Gray
Cuvier's Beaked Whale	Ballena picuda de Cuvier
S. Bottlenose Whale	Ballena nariz de botella
Long-finned Pilot Whale	Ballena piloto
Killer Whale (Orca)	Orca
Sperm Whale	Cachalote
Antarctic Minke Whale	Ballena minke
Dwarf Minke Whale	Ballena minke enana
Sei Whale	Ballena sei
Fin Whale	Ballena de aleta
Blue Whale	Ballena azul
Humpback Whale	Ballena jorobada
Southern Right Whale	Ballena franca austral
Pygmy Right Whale	Ballena franca pigmea
European Rabbit	Conejo
Norway Rat	Guarén
Feral Cat	Gato doméstico silvestre
Marine Otter	Chungungo
Patagonian Gray Fox	Chilla
Auckland Pig	Jabalí
Guanaco	Guanaco
Reindeer	Reno
Mouflon	Muflón

FALKLAND BREEDING BIRDS

White-tufted Grebe	Pimpollo
Silvery Grebe	Blanquillo
Imperial (King) Shag	Cormorán imperial
Rock Shag	Cormorán de las rocas
Bk-crowned Night-Heron	Huairavo
Coscoroba Swan	Cisne coscoroba
Black-necked Swan	Cisne de cuello negro
Feral Domestic Goose	Ganso doméstico silvestre
Upland Goose	Caiquén
Kelp Goose	Caranca
Ruddy-headed Goose	Canquén colorado
Ashy-headed Goose	Canquén
Falkland Steamerduck	Quetru de las Falklands
Flying Steamerduck	Quetru volador
Pat. Crested Duck	Pato juarjual
Chloe Wigeon	Pato real
Cinnamon Teal	Pato colorado
Red Shoveler	Pato cuchara
Yellow-billed Pintail	Pato jergón grande
Speckled Teal	Pato jergón chico
Silver Teal	Pato capuchino
Turkey Vulture	Jote de cabeza colorada
Red-backed Hawk	Aguilucho
Striated Caracara	Carancho negro
Crested Caracara	Carancho
Peregrine Falcon	Halcón peregrino
American Kestrel	Cernícalo
Magellan Oystercatcher	Pilpilén austral
Blackish Oystercatcher	Pilpilén negro
Two-banded Plover	Chorlo de doble collar
Rufous-chested Dotterel	Chorlo chileno
Magellanic Snipe	Becasina
Least Seedsnipe	Perdicita
Falkland Skua	Salteador de las Falklands
Dolphin Gull	Gaviota austral
Brown-hooded Gull	Gaviota cáhuil
South American Tern	Gaviotín sudamericano
Barn Owl	Lechuza
Short-eared Owl	Nuco
Blackish Cinclodes	Churrete austral
D.-faced Ground-Tyrant	Dormilona tontita
Chilean Swallow	Golondrina chilena
Falkland Pipit	Bailarín chico
Falkland Thrush	Zorzal
Grass Wren	Chercán de las vegas
Cobb's Wren	Chercán de Cobb
Long-tailed Meadowlark	Loica
Black-chinned Siskin	Jilguero
Black-throated Finch	Yal austral

GERMAN NAMES

PENGUINS

Adélie Penguin	Adéliepinguin
Gentoo Penguin	Eselspinguin
Chinstrap Penguin	Zügelpinguin
Emperor Penguin	Kaiserpinguin
King Penguin	Königspinguin
Rockhopper Penguin	Felsenpinguin
Macaroni Penguin	Goldschopfpinguin
Royal Penguin	Haubenpinguin
Snares Penguin	Snares-Dickschnabelpinguin
Erect-crested Penguin	Kronenpinguin
Fiordland Penguin	Dickschnabelpinguin
Yellow-eyed Penguin	Gelbaugenpinguin
Magellanic Penguin	Magellanpinguin
Humboldt Penguin	Humboldtpinguin
African Penguin	Brillenpinguin
Galapagos Penguin	Galapagospinguin
Little Penguin	Zwergpinguin

ALBATROSSES

Wandering Albatross	Wanderalbatros
Royal Albatross	Königsalbatros
Black-browed Albatross	Schwarzbrauenalbatros
Shy Albatross	Weisskappenalbatros
Gray-headed Albatross	Graukopfalbatros
Buller's Albatross	Bulleralbatros
Yellow-nosed Albatross	Gelbnasenalbatros
Lt-mantle Sooty Albatross	Russalbatros
Sooty Albatross	Dunkelalbatros

PETRELS

Southern Giant-Petrel	Südlicher Riesensturmvogel
Northern Giant-Petrel	Nördlicher Riesensturmvogel
Southern Fulmar	Silbersturmvogel
Antarctic Petrel	Weissflügelsturmvogel
Cape Petrel	Kapsturmvogel
Snow Petrel	Schneesturmvogel
White-headed Petrel	Weisskopfsturmvogel
Mottled Petrel	Regensturmvogel
Great-winged Petrel	Langflügelsturmvogel
Kerguelen Petrel	Kerguelensturmvogel
Atlantic Petrel	Schlegelsturmvogel
Soft-plumaged Petrel	Weichfedersturmvogel
White-chinned Petrel	Weisskinnsturmvogel
Gray Petrel	Grausturmvogel
Greater Shearwater	Kappensturmtaucher
Flesh-footed Shearwater	Blassfusssturmtaucher
Sooty Shearwater	Dunkelsturmtaucher
Short-tailed Shearwater	Kurzschwanz-Sturmtaucher
Little Shearwater	Kleiner-Sturmtaucher
Broad-billed Prion	Grosser-Entensturmvogel
Salvin's Prion	Kleiner-Entensturmvogel
Antarctic Prion	Taubensturmvogel
Slender-billed Prion	Belcher-Sturmvogel
Fairy Prion	Feensturmvogel
Fulmar Prion	Dickschnabelsturmvogel
Blue Petrel	Blausturmvogel

STORM-PETRELS

Wilson's Storm-Petrel	Buntfuss-Sturmschwalbe
Gray-backed Storm-Petrel	Graurücken-Sturmschwalbe
White-faced Storm-Petrel	Weissgesicht-Sturmschwalbe
Black-bellied Storm-Petrel	Schwarzbauchmeerläufer
White-bellied Storm-Petrel	Weissbauchmeerläufer

DIVING-PETRELS

Common Diving-Petrel	Lummensturmvogel
SG Diving-Petrel	Südgeorgien-Lummensturmvogel

CORMORANTS

Antarctic Shag	Blauaugenscharbe
South Georgian Shag	Südgeorgienscharbe
Macquarie Shag	Macquariescharbe
Kerguelen Shag	Kerguelenscharbe
Crozet Shag	Crozetscharbe
Heard Shag	Heardscharbe
Campbell Shag	Campbellscharbe
Auckland Shag	Aucklandscharbe
Bounty Shag	Bountyscharbe

WATERFOWL

Australian Shelduck	Halsbandkasarka
Mallard	Stockente
Pacific Black Duck	Augenbrauenente
Auckland Flightless Teal	Aucklandente
Campbell Flightless Teal	Campbellente
Eaton's Pintail	Eatonente
South Georgia Pintail	Südgeorgien-Spitzschwanzente
Speckled Teal	Andenente
Auckland Merganser	Aucklandsäger

FALCONS

New Zealand Falcon	Maori-Falke

RAILS

Gough Moorhen	Tristanteichhuhn
Auckland Island Rail	Aucklandralle
Inaccessible Flightless Rail	Atlantisralle

SHEATHBILLS

Snowy Sheathbill	Weissgesicht-Scheidenschnabel
Black-faced Sheathbill	Schwarzgesicht-Scheidenschnabel

SHOREBIRDS

Double-banded Dotterel	Doppelband-Regenpfeifer
New Zealand Snipe	Aucklandschnepfe

GULLS, TERNS & SKUAS

Kelp Gull	Dominikanermöwe
Red-Billed Gull	Rotschnabelmöwe
Common Noddy	Noddi
Antarctic Tern	Antipodenseeschwalbe
Arctic Tern	Küstenseeschwalbe
White-fronted Tern	Kerguelenseeschwalbe
Sooty Tern	Russseeschwalbe
South Polar Skua	Südpolarskua
Brown Skua	Braunskua

PARAKEETS

Antipodes Parakeet	Einfarbsittich
Red-crowned Parakeet	Ziegensittich
Yellow-crowned Parakeet	Springsittich

PASSERINES

South Georgia Pipit	Riesenpieper
New Zealand Pipit	Spornpieper
New Zealand Bellbird	Makomako
Tui	Tui
Tristan Thrush	Tristandrossel
European Blackbird	Amsel
Song Thrush	Singdrossel
Auckland Tomtit	Maorischnäpper
Snares Tomtit	Snares-Maorischnäpper
Snares Fernbird	Farnsteiger
New Zealand Fantail	Grau-Fächerschwanz
Silvereye	Mantel-Brillenvogel
Skylark	Feldlerche
Common Starling	Star
Dunnock	Hecken-Braunelle
Common Chaffinch	Buchfink
European Goldfinch	Distelfink
Common Redpoll	Birkenzeisig
Yellowhammer	Goldammer
House Sparrow	Haussperling
Gough Bunting	Gough-Rowettia
Tristan Bunting	Tristanammernfink
Grosbeak Bunting	Wilkins-Ammernfink

MAMMALS

New Zealand Sea Lion	Auckland-Seelöwe
Antarctic Fur Seal	Antarktis-Seebär
Subantarctic Fur Seal	Subantarktis-Seebär
New Zealand Fur Seal	Neuseeland-Seebär
South American Fur Seal	Südamerikanischer-Seebär
South African Fur Seal	Südafrikanischer-Seebär
Southern Elephant Seal	Südlicher-Seelefant
Weddell Seal	Weddellrobbe
Crabeater Seal	Krabbenfresserrobbe
Ross Seal	Rossrobbe
Leopard Seal	Seeleopard
Commerson's Dolphin	Commersondelphin
Hourglass Dolphin	Stundenglassdelphin
Dusky Dolphin	Schwarzdelphin
Peale's Dolphin	Pealesdelphin
Bottlenose Dolphin	Grosser-Tümmler
Spectacled Porpoise	Brillenschweinswal
Arnoux's Beaked Whale	Südlicher-Glattdelphin
S. Right Whale Dolphin	Südlicher-Schwarzwal
Strap-toothed Whale	Layardwal
Gray's Beaked Whale	Gray-Zweizahnwal
Cuvier's Beaked Whale	Cuvier-Schnabelwal
S. Bottlenose Whale	Südlicher-Entenwal
Long-finned Pilot Whale	Grindwal
Killer Whale (Orca)	Schwertwal
Sperm Whale	Pottwal
Antarctic Minke Whale	Zwergwal
Dwarf Minke Whale	Kleiner-Zwergwal
Sei Whale	Seiwal
Fin Whale	Finwal
Blue Whale	Blauwal
Humpback Whale	Buckelwal
Southern Right Whale	Südlicherglattwal
Pygmy Right Whale	Zwergglattwal
European Rabbit	Kaninchen
Norway Rat	Norwegische-Ratte
Feral Cat	Wildkatze
Marine Otter	Meerotter
Patagonian Gray Fox	Patagonischer-Graufuchs
Auckland Pig	Auckland-Wildschwein
Guanaco	Guanaco
Reindeer	Rentier
Mouflon	Mufflon

FALKLAND BREEDING BIRDS

White-tufted Grebe	Rolland-Taucher
Silvery Grebe	Inka-Taucher
Imperial (King) Shag	Königskormoran
Rock Shag	Felsenkormoran
Bk-crowned Night-Heron	Schwarzkronen-Nachtreiher
Coscoroba Swan	Coscoroba-Schwan
Black-necked Swan	Schwarzhals-Schwan
Upland Goose	Magellangans
Feral Domestic Goose	Graugans
Kelp Goose	Kelpgans
Ruddy-headed Goose	Rotkopfgans
Ashy-headed Goose	Graukopfgans
Falkland Steamerduck	Flugunfähige-Dampfschiffente
Flying Steamerduck	Dampfschiffente
Patagonian Crested Duck	Schopfente
Chiloe Wigeon	Chilenische-Pfeifente
Cinnamon Teal	Zimtente
Red Shoveler	Fuchs-Löffelente
Yellow-billed Pintail	Georgische-Spitzschwanzente
Speckled Teal	Andenente
Silver Teal	Silberente
Turkey Vulture	Truthahngeier
Red-backed Hawk	Rotrückenbussard
Striated Caracara	Falkland-Caracara
Crested Caracara	Hauben-Caracara
Peregrine Falcon	Wanderfalke
American Kestrel	Buntfalke
Magellanic Oystercatcher	Magellan-Austernfischer
Blackish Oystercatcher	Russ-Austernfischer
Two-banded Plover	Zweiband-Regenpfeifer
Rufous-chested Dotterel	Rotbrustregenpfeifer
Magellanic Snipe	Magellanschnepfe
Least Seedsnipe	Zwerg-Höhenläufer
Falkland Skua	Falkland-Skua
Dolphin Gull	Blutschnabelmöwe
Brown-hooded Gull	Patagonienmöwe
South American Tern	Südamerikanischeseeschwalbe
Barn Owl	Schleiereule
Short-eared Owl	Sumpfohreule
Blackish Cinclodes	Tussockvogel
Dark-faced Ground-Tyrant	Maskentyran
Chilean Swallow	Chile-Schwalbe
Falkland Pipit	Falkland-Pieper
Falkland Thrush	Falkland-Drossel
Grass Wren	Seggen-Zaunkönig
Cobb's Wren	Südlicher-Hauszaunkönig
Long-tailed Meadowlark	Soldatenstärling
Black-chinned Siskin	Bartzeisig
Black-throated Finch	Schwarzkehlfink

PENGUINS

Adélie Penguin	Manchot adélie
Gentoo Penguin	Manchot papou
Chinstrap Penguin	Manchot à jugulaire
Emperor Penguin	Manchot empereur
King Penguin	Manchot royal
Rockhopper Penguin	Gorfou sauteur
Macaroni Penguin	Gorfou macaroni
Royal Penguin	Gorfou de Schlegel
Snares Penguin	Gorfou des îles Snares
Erect-crested Penguin	Gorfou de Sclater
Fiordland Penguin	Gorfou de Fjordland
Yellow-eyed Penguin	Manchot à oeil jaune
Magellanic Penguin	Manchot de Magellan
Humboldt Penguin	Manchot de Humboldt
African Penguin	Manchot du cap
Galapagos Penguin	Manchot des Galapagos
Little Penguin	Manchot pygmée

ALBATROSSES

English	French
Wandering Albatross	Grand albatros
Royal Albatross	Albatros royal
Black-browed Albatross	Albatros à sourcils noirs
Shy Albatross	Albatros timide
Gray-headed Albatross	Albatros à tête grise
Buller's Albatross	Albatros de Buller
Yellow-nosed Albatross	Albatros à bec jaune
Lt-mantle Sooty Albatross	Albatros fuligineux à dos clair
Sooty Albatross	A. fuligineux à dos sombre

PETRELS

English	French
Southern Giant-Petrel	Pétrel géant antarctique
Northern Giant-Petrel	Pétrel géant subantarctique
Southern Fulmar	Fulmar antarctique
Antarctic Petrel	Pétrel antarctique
Cape Petrel	Damier du Cap
Snow Petrel	Pétrel des neiges
Broad-billed Prion	Prion de Forster
Antarctic Prion	Prion de Salvin
Slender-billed Prion	Prion de la désolation
Fairy Prion	Prion de Belcher
Fulmar Prion	prion prion
Blue Petrel	Pétrel bleu

STORM-PETRELS

English	French
Wilson's Storm-Petrel	Pétrel-tempête de Wilson
Gray-backed Storm-Petrel	Pétrel-tempête à croupion gris
White-faced Storm-Petrel	Océanite frégate
Black-bellied Storm-Petrel	Pétrel-tempête à ventre noir
White-bellied Storm-Petrel	Pétrel-tempête à ventre blanc

DIVING-PETRELS

English	French
S Georgian Diving-Petrel	P. plongeur de Géorgie du sud
Common Diving-Petrel	Pétrel plongeur commun

CORMORANTS

English	French
Antarctic Shag	Cormoran antarctique
South Georgian Shag	Cormoran de Géorgie du sud
Macquarie Shag	Cormoran de Macquarie
Kerguelen Shag	Cormoran des Kerguelen
Crozet Shag	Cormoran de Crozet
Heard Shag	Cormoran de l'île Heard
Campbell Shag	Cormoran des îles Campbell
Auckland Shag	Cormoran des îles Auckland
Bounty Shag	Cormoran des îles Bounty

WATERFOWL

English	French
Australasian Shelduck	Tadorne d'Australie
Mallard	Canard colvert
Pacific Black Duck	Canard à sourcils
Auckland Flightless Teal	Sarcelle d'Auckland
Campbell Flightless Teal	Sarcelle brune
Eaton's Pintail	Canard d'Eaton
South Georgia Teal	Canard de Géorgie du sud
Speckled Teal	Sarcelle à bec jaune
Auckland Merganser	Harle de l'île Auckland

FALCONS

English	French
New Zealand Falcon	Faucon de Nouvelle-Zélande

RAILS

English	French
Gough Moorhen	Gallinule de Tristan
Auckland Island Rail	Râle d'Auckland
Inaccessible Flightless Rail	Râle Atlantis

SHEATHBILLS

English	French
Snowy Sheathbill	Grand Bec-en-Fourreau
Black-faced Sheathbill	Petit Bec-en-Fourreau

SHOREBIRDS

English	French
Double-banded Dotterel	Pluvier à double collier
New Zealand Snipe	Bécassine d'auckland

GULLS, TERNS & SKUAS

English	French
Kelp Gull	Goéland dominicain
Red-billed Gull	Mouette scopuline
Common Noddy	Noddi brun
Antarctic Tern	Sterne antarctique
Arctic Tern	Sterne arctique
Kerguelen Tern	Sterne de Kerguelen
White-fronted Tern	Sterne Tara
Sooty Tern	Sterne fuligineuse
South Polar Skua	Skua antarctique
Brown Skua	Skua subantarctique

PARAKEETS

English	French
Antipodes Parakeet	Perruche des Antipodes
Red-crowned Parakeet	Perruche de Sparrman
Yellow-crowned Parakeet	Perruche à tête d'or

PASSERINES

English	French
South Georgia Pipit	Pipit de Géorgie du sud
New Zealand Pipit	Pipit de Nouvelle-Zélande
New Zealand Bellbird	Méliphage carillonneur
Tui	Tui à Cravatte frisée
Tristan Thrush	Grive de Tristan da Cunha
European Blackbird	Merle noir
Song Thrush	Grive musicienne
Auckland Tomtit	Miro des îles Auckland
Snares Tomtit	Miro des îles Snares
New Zealand Fantail	Rhipidure à collier
Silvereye	Zostérops à dos gris
Skylark	Alouette des champs
Common Starling	Étourneau sansonnet
Dunnock	Accenteur mouchet
Common Chaffinch	Pinson des arbres
European Goldfinch	Chardonneret élégant
Common Redpoll	Sizerin flammé
Yellowhammer	Bruant jaune
House Sparrow	Moineau domestique
Gough Bunting	Rowettie de Gough
Tristan Bunting	Nésospize acunha
Grosbeak Bunting	Nésospize de Wilkins

MAMMALS

English	French
New Zealand Sea Lion	Lion de mer de Hooker
South American Sea Lion	Lion de mer austral
Antarctic Fur Seal	Otarie à fourrure antarctique
Subantarctic Fur Seal	O. à fourrure subantarctique
South African Fur Seal	O. à fourrure d'Afrique du sud
New-Zealand fur Seal	O. à fourrure de N. Zélande
Southern Elephant Seal	Éléphant de mer austral
Weddell Seal	Phoque de Weddell
Crabeater Seal	Phoque crabier
Ross Seal	Phoque de Ross
Leopard Seal	Léopard de mer
Commerson's Dolphin	Dauphin de Commerson
Hourglass Dolphin	Lagénorhynque croisé
Dusky Dolphin	Lagénorhynque obscur
Peale's Dolphin	Lagénorhynque de Peale
Bottlenose Dolphin	Grand dauphin
Spectacled Porpoise	Marsouin à lunettes
Arnoux's Beaked Whale	Bérardius austral
Strap-toothed Whale	Mésoplodon de Layard
Gray's Beaked Whale	Mésoplodon de Gray
Cuvier's Beaked Whale	Ziphius
S. Bottlenose Whale	Hyperoodon antarctique
Long-finned Pilot Whale	Globicéphale noir
Killer Whale (Orca)	Orque épaulard
Sperm Whale	Grand Cachalot
Antarctic Minke Whale	Petit rorqual antarctique
Dwarf Minke Whale	Petit rorqual à museau pointu
Sei Whale	Rorqual boréal
Fin Whale	Rorqual commun
Blue Whale	Baleine bleue
Humpback Whale	Baleine à bosses
S. Right Whale	Baleine franche australe
Pygmy Right Whale	Baleine franche pygmée
European Rabbit	Lapin de Garenne
Norway Rat	Rat surmulot
Feral Cat	Chat haret
Marine Otter	Loutre féline
Patagonian Gray Fox	Renard gris de Patagonie
Wild Pig	Sanglier
Guanaco	Guanaco
Reindeer	Renne
Mouflon	Mouflon

FALKLAND BREEDING BIRDS

English	French
White-tufted Grebe	Grèbe de Rolland
Silvery Grebe	Grèbe aux belles joues
Imperial (King) Shag	Cormoran impérial
Rock Shag	Cormoran de Magellan
Bk-crowned Night-Heron	Bihoreau gris
Coscoroba Swan	Cygne de Coscoroba
Black-necked Swan	Cygne à cou noir
Feral Domestic Goose	Oie cendrée
Upland Goose	Ouette de Magellan
Kelp Goose	Ouette marine
Ruddy-headed Goose	Ouette à tête rousse
Ashy-headed Goose	Ouette à tête grise
Falkland Steamerduck	Canard-vapeur des Malouines
Flying Steamerduck	Canard-vapeur de Patagonie
Patagonian Crested Duck	Harle couronné de Patagonie
Chiloe Wigeon	Canard de Chiloé
Mallard	Canard colvert
Argentine Cinnamon Teal	Sarcelle cannelle
Red Shoveler	Canard spatule
Speckled Teal	Sarcelle à bec jaune
Silver Teal	Sarcelle bariolée
Turkey Vulture	Urubu à tête rouge
Red-Backed Hawk	Buse tricolore
Striated Caracara	Caracara austral
Crested Caracara	Caracara huppé
Peregrine Falcon	Faucon pèlerin
American Kestrel	Crécerelle d'Amérique
Magellanic Oystercatcher	Huîtrier de Garnot
Blackish Oystercatcher	Huîtrier noir
Two-banded Plover	Pluvier d'Urville
Rufous-chested Dotterel	Pluvier des Falkland
Magellanic Snipe	Bécassine de Magellan
Least Seedsnipe	Thinocore de Patagonie
Brown Skua	Skua subantarctique
Kelp Gull	Goéland dominicain
Dolphin Gull	Goéland de Scoresby
Brown-hooded Gull	Mouette de Patagonie
South American Tern	Sterne sud-américaine
Barn Owl	Chouette effraie
Short-Eared Owl	Hibou des marais
Blackish Cinclodes	Cinclode noir
Dark-Faced Ground Tyrant	Dormilon bistré
Chilean Swallow	Hirondelle du Chili
Correndera Pipit	Pipit correndera
Falkland Thrush	Grive des Malouines
Grass Wren	Troglodyte à bec court
Cobb's Wren	Troglodyte de Cobb
Long-Tailed Meadowlark	Sturnelle australe
House Sparrow	Moineau domestique
Black-chinned Siskin	Chardonneret à menton noir
Black-throated Finch	Mélanodère à sourcils blancs

Albatross, Amsterdam 20
  Black-browed 23
  Buller's 25
  Chatham 22
  Gray-headed 24
  Laysan 66
  Light-mantled Sooty 27
  Royal 19,20
  Salvin's 22
  Shy 21
  Sooty 28
  Wandering 16,17,18
  White-capped 21
  Yellow-nosed 26
Bat, Brazilian Free-tailed 76
Bellbird, New Zealand 62
Blackbird, European 64
Boobook, Southern 75
Bronze-Cuckoo, Shining 75
Bunting, Gough 63
  Grosbeak 63
  Tristan 63
Canastero, Austral 132
Caracara, Chimango 125
  Crested 111
  Striated 111
Cat, Feral 97
Chaffinch, Common 65
Chat, Mountain 75
Cinclodes, Bar-winged 130
  Blackish (Tussockbird) . . . 117
Coot, Eurasian 68
  Red-fronted 125
  Red-gartered 132
  White-winged 125
Cormorant, Great 74
  Little Pied 67
  Pied 74
  Red-legged 122
Corncrake 74
Crake, Baillon's 74
  Paint-billed 74
Cuckoo, Common 72
  Dark-billed 132
  Lesser 75
  Long-tailed 75
  Oriental 75
  Pallid 75

Cuckoo, Red-chested 75
Curlew, Eskimo 132
Diucon, Fire-eyed 131
Diving-Petrel, Common 45
  Magellanic 132
  South Georgian 45
Dolphin, Bottlenose 85
  Commerson's 83
  Dusky 84
  Hourglass 83
  Peale's 84
  Southern Right Whale 86
Dotterel, Double-banded 54
  Rufous-chested 74,114
  Tawny-throated 126
Dove, Eared 130
Duck, Black-headed 124
  Lake 74,124
  Maned 68
  Pacific Black 49
  Patagonian Crested 107
  Spectacled 123
Dunnock 65
Egret, Cattle 67
  Great 67
  Intermediate 74
  Snowy 67
Elaenia, White-crested 132
Falcon, Aplomado 125
  New Zealand 52
  Peregrine 74,112
Fantail, New Zealand 61
Fernbird, Snares Island 62
Finch, Black-throated 119
  Yellow-bridled 132
Firecrown, Green-backed . . . 132
Flamingo, Chilean 123
Flycatcher, Fork-tailed 132
Fox, Gray 97
Fulmar, Southern 30
Gallinule, Purple 69
Gannet, Australasian 74
  Cape 66
Giant-Petrel, Northern 28
  Southern 29
Godwit, Bar-tailed 74
  Black-tailed 70
  Hudsonian 74,132

Golden-Plover, American . . . 126
Goldfinch, European 65
Goose, Ashy-headed 105
  Canada 67
  Domestic 103
  Kelp 104
  Ruddy-headed 105
  Upland 103
Grebe, Great 122
  Pied-billed 122
  Silvery 100
  White-tufted 100
  Hoary-headed 74
Greenfinch, European 73
Greenshank, Common 74
Ground-Dove, Ruddy 132
Ground-Tyrant, Dark-faced . 118
  White-browed 132
Guanaco 98
Gull, Band-tailed 128
  Black-billed 72
  Brown-hooded 115
  Dolphin 115
  Franklin's 74,132
  Gray 128
  Gray-headed 132
  Hartlaub's 75
  Kelp 56
  Lesser Black-backed 72
  Red-billed 55
  Sabine's 75
  Yellow-legged 75
Hare, European 76
Harrier, Cinereous 125
  Long-winged 132
  Swamp 74
Hawk, Red-backed 110
  Sharp-shinned 124
Heron, Cocoi 74,122
  Striated 66
  White-faced 67
Hobby, Eurasian 74
Ibis, Black-faced 123
Jaeger, Long-tailed 129
  Parasitic 72
  Pomarine 72
Kestrel, American 112
Kingbird, Eastern 131

Kiskadee, Great 131
Knot, Red 70
Lapwing, Blacksmith 74
Southern 126
Spur-winged 74
Masked 69
Mallard 64
Martin, Brown-chested 132
House 75
Purple 132
Sand 75,133
Southern 132
Tree 75
Meadowlark, Long-tailed 75,118
Merganser, Auckland 49
Mockingbird, Patagonian . . . 132
Moorhen, Gough 53
Mouflon 98
Mouse, House 76
Needletail, White-throated . . . 75
Negrito, Austral 75,130
Nighthawk, Common 73
Night-Heron, Bk-crowned . . 100
Noddy, Common 56
Otter, Marine 97
Owl, Barn 75,117
Burrowing 129
Magellanic Horned 129
Rufous-legged 132
Short-eared 117
Oystercatcher, Blackish 113
Magellanic 113
Pied 72
Parakeet, Antipodes 60
Austral 129
Red-crowned 60
Yellow-crowned 60
Parrot, Burrowing 129
Penguin, Adélie 5
African 13
Chinstrap 7
Emperor 4
Erect-crested 11
Fiordland 12
Galapagos 14
Gentoo 7
Humboldt 14
King 5

Penguin, Little 14,15
Macaroni 10
Magellanic 13
Rockhopper 8,9
Royal 10
Snares 11
Yellow-eyed 12
Petrel, Antarctic 30
Atlantic 33
Blue 42
Cape 31
Gray 35
Great-winged 34
Herald 132
Kerguelen 35
Mottled 33
Snow 31
Soft-plumaged 34
Spectacled 36
White-chinned 36
White-headed 32
Phalarope, Red 71
Wilson's 71
Pig 98
Pigeon, Chilean 132
Pintail, Eaton's 51,74
South Georgia 51,74
White-cheeked 124
Yellow-billed 74,109
Pipit, Auckland 61
Falkland (Correndera) 117
South Georgia 61
Plantcutter, Rufous-tailed . . . 132
Plover, Black-bellied 69
Magellanic 127
Ringed 69
Three-banded 74
Two-banded 114
Pochard, Rosy-billed 123
Porpoise, Spectacled 85
Prion, Antarctic 39
Broad-billed 40
Fairy 41
Fulmar 41
Salvin's 39
Slender-billed 40
Rabbit, European 97
Rail, Auckland Island 52

Rail, Austral 126
Inaccessible Island 52
Plumbeous 126
Speckled 132
Weka 68
Rat, Black 76
Norway 76,97
Rayadito, Thorn-tailed 130
Redpoll, Common 64
Reindeer 98
Roller, Broad-billed 73
Sanderling 71
Sandpiper, Baird's 74,127
Common 75
Curlew 75
Least 74
Pectoral 71
Semipalmated 132
Sharp-tailed 75
Solitary 74
Spotted 70
Stilt 132
Terek 75
Upland 70
White-rumped 71
Wood 74
Sandplover, Greater 74
Sea Lion, New Zealand 77
South American 77
Seal, Antarctic Fur 78
Crabeater 81
Leopard 82
New Zealand Fur 79
Ross 81
South African Fur 79
South American Fur 79
Southern Elephant 80
Subantarctic Fur 78
Weddell 80
Seedsnipe, Least 75,113
White-bellied 132
Shag, Antarctic 45
Auckland 48
Bounty 48
Campbell 48
Crozet 47
Heard 46
Imperial/King 101

Shag, Kerguelen 46
Macquarie 46
Rock 101
South Georgian 47
Shearwater, Cory's 132
Flesh-footed 37
Greater 37
Little 37
Manx 132
Short-tailed 38
Sooty 38
Sheathbill, Black-faced 53
Snowy 54
Shelduck, Australian 49
Shoveler, Red 108
Shrike, Red-backed 73
Shrike-Tyrant, Black-billed . 132
Sierra-Finch, Gray-hooded . . 132
Mourning 132
Patagonian 132
Silvereye 63
Siskin, Black-chinned 119
Skua, Brown (Subantarctic) . . 59
Chilean 128
Falkland 116
South Polar 58
Skylark 65
Snipe, Cordilleran 99
Latham's 74
Magellanic 113
New Zealand 55
Sparrow, House 65
Rufous-collared 131
Spoonbill, Roseate 123
Starling, Common 65
Steamerduck, Falkland 106
Flying 106
Stilt, Black-necked 127
White-headed 71
Stint, Little 75
Red-necked 75
Stork, Maguari 122
White 67
Storm-Petrel, Black-bellied . . 44
European 132
Gray-backed 43
Leach's 74
White-bellied 44

Storm-petrel, White-faced . . . 43
Wilson's 42
Surfbird 127
Swallow, Barn 73
Blue-and-White 132
Chilean 75,118
Cliff 131
Southern Rough-winged . . 132
Tawny-headed 132
Welcome 73
White-rumped 132
Swamphen, Purple 69
Swan, Black-necked 74,103
Coscoroba 102a
Swift, Ashy-tailed 132
Common 75
Fork-tailed 75
White-collared 132
Tapaculo, Magellanic 132
Tattler, Gray-tailed 75
Teal, Auckland 50
Blue-winged 68
Campbell 50
Cinnamon 74,108
Gray 68
Silver 108
Speckled 49,74,109
Tern, Antarctic 57
Arctic 57
Black-fronted 75
Common 128
Elegant 128
Kerguelen 58
Sandwich 128
Sooty 57
South American 116
Trudeau's 132
White-fronted 56
Thrush, Falkland 118
Song 64
Tristan 61
Wood 132
Tit-Tyrant, Tufted 132
Tomtit, Auckland Island 62
Snares Island 62
Tui 62
Turnstone, Ruddy 70
Turtle-Dove, Cape 75

Turtle-Dove, European 75
Laughing 75
Tussockbird 117
Tyrant, Cattle 130
Vulture, Turkey 74,109
Wagtail, Yellow 75
Warbler, Gray 73
Willow 75
Waxbill, Common 75
Whale, Andrew's Beaked 76
Antarctic Minke 92
Arnoux's Beaked 87
Blue 94
Cuvier's Beaked 88
Dwarf Minke 91
Fin 93
Gray's Beaked 87
Hector's Beaked 76
Humpback 95
Killer (Orca) 89
Long-finned Pilot 86
Pygmy Right 91
Sei 93
Shepherd's Beaked 76
Southern Bottlenose 87
Southern Right 96
Sperm 90
Strap-toothed 88
Whimbrel 70
Whitethroat, Common 75
Wigeon, Chiloe 107
Wren, Cobb's 119
Grass 119
Yellowhammer 64
Yellowlegs, Greater 127
Lesser 132